PM Crash Course™

PM Crash Course™

PM *CRASH COURSE*™

A Revolutionary Guide to What REALLY Matters
When Managing Projects

To all those brave enough to try to make a difference in their world and thereby make the whole world a better place. You honor me by reading this book and telling others about it. Now let's see what happens when you use what you learn!

Printed in the United States of America

ISBN: 1-932735-07-0

Library of Congress Control Number: 2006937299

RMC Publications, Inc.
Phone: 952.846.4484
Fax: 952.846.4844
E-mail: info@rmcproject.com
Web: www.rmcproject.com

Table of Contents

	Introduction to the Premier Edition of PM Crash Course™	ix
Chapter 1:	Before You Read This Book	1
Chapter 2:	How to Use This Book	5
Chapter 3:	Understanding the Project Management Process	9
Chapter 4:	Finalizing What Is Asked of You—The Project Charter	21
Chapter 5:	Breaking the Work into Projects	33
Chapter 6:	Gaining, Creating, and Using Historical Information	41
Chapter 7:	Identifying and Managing Stakeholders	49
Chapter 8:	Finalizing Project Objectives— The Project Scope Statement	73
Chapter 9:	Preventing Scope Creep— The Work Breakdown Structure and WBS Dictionary	89
Chapter 10:	Real-World Estimating	117
Chapter 11:	Real-World Scheduling	129
Chapter 12:	Communications Management	145
Chapter 13:	Preventing Problems Rather Than Just Dealing with Them—Risk Management	163
Chapter 14:	Common Errors That Can Ruin Your Career	175
Chapter 15:	Nine Things Your Boss Should Be Doing	177
Chapter 16:	What to Learn Next	179
	Index	185

About the Author

Rita Mulcahy is an internationally recognized expert on project management techniques, advanced project management theory, risk management, and project management certification.

She is the founder and CEO of RMC Project Management, one of the fastest-growing project management training organizations in the world.

Rita has over 15 years and US $2.5 billion worth of hands-on project experience. She has turned this experience into more than 10 best-selling project management resources, which have helped over 150,000 people manage their projects better. Rita has a reputation for helping people to learn and to have fun while doing it.

Her project management courses are taught in over 13 countries around the globe, and her products are used in more than 40 countries.

About RMC Project Management

RMC Project Management is a global project management training company, specializing in real-world project management training. The company's focus is helping project managers use the latest project management tools and techniques to complete projects faster—and with less expense, better results, and fewer resources. RMC provides training for the entire project management career path, from basic project management to professional certification training, and advanced project management training. Its classes are targeted toward team members, project managers, project management offices, and senior management, and include the following:

- PM Crash Course™ (1 day)

- Project Management Tricks of the Trade® (3 days)

- Tricks of the Trade® for Risk Management (2 days)

- What Makes a Project Manager Successful? (2 days)

- Tricks of the Trade® for Negotiation (2 days)

- Understanding Contracts (2 days)

- Tricks of the Trade® for Determining Project Requirements (1 day)

- Why Projects Fail and How to Prevent Failure (1/2 - 1 day)

- Tricks for Avoiding Common Project Problems (1/2 - 1 day)

- Common Risk Management Errors That Can Ruin Your Career (1/2 day)

- Executive Briefing on Project Management (1 day)

- Professional Certification Preparation (2 to 4 days)

RMC's latest series of professional development resources corresponding to this RMC book will include a classroom-based course, an e-Learning application, project manager evaluation software, and a number of other helpful products.

Introduction to the Premier Edition of PM Crash Course™

By Rita Mulcahy

The fact that you are reading this book indicates that you realize it is time for a change. It is time to make a difference in how your projects have been going and how your own career in project management is progressing. You have an idea of what project management is…. but are your perceptions accurate? Do you know that project management is a science AND an art? Do you have any idea of the difference good project management can make on your projects? Do you realize that there are key things that you should do and not do?

Be warned, this book does not cover all aspects of project management. The scope of this book is to show you the tricks of where to focus your project management efforts to make the greatest immediate impact. It is intended for people like you, who, for whatever reason, find themselves responsible for completing a project, but do not have formal project management training. If you were to ask me, "As an innovator in project management training for so many years, what do you think are the most important things I need to know in order to make a difference on my project RIGHT NOW?" this book would be my response.

I will help you start controlling your projects rather than allowing them to control you. The end result of reading this book will be projects that are completed faster, cheaper, and easier. And of course, your reputation as a project manager will benefit immensely as well.

This book may whet your appetite to learn about project management in more depth. If so, this could be the start of a long relationship between you and my company, RMC Project Management. At RMC, we can help you explore the intricacies of this exciting field in much more detail. For example, you might gain some free Tricks of the Trade® or participate in a project management contest by visiting our Web site, www.rmcproject.com. Maybe you will continue your project management education by attending our one-day instructor-led course titled PM Crash Course™, covering the topics in this book in the real world. Or, you may choose to take that course online! If getting more advanced training interests you, RMC has many publicly offered courses. There's a very good chance that one of them will be just what you need in order to take the next step. Someday, you may decide to pursue certification in the field of project management. We can help you with that as well—whether you choose to self-study, take a class, or participate in a course online. Our training methodology in project management is second to none and used in over 40 countries for a very good reason: it's the best there is.

In any case, this book is an excellent place to start.

What are we waiting for? Let's get going.

Did you know there are secrets to success in project management? No matter how long you have worked on projects or how much you already know, there are many more secrets for you to learn. Most project managers have spent many years "learning" project management, only to discover that they do not know what they really NEED to know; only to discover no change in the success of their projects.

This book is designed to teach you the things you absolutely must know to successfully manage projects in the real world…. and nothing else. Just real-world tools that you can begin using on your projects immediately.

Look around you at work. Most people rarely get a chance to make a difference. Projects, on the other hand, are designed to make a change, make a difference, and make things better within your environment. Time spent learning more about this profession can help you increase the difference you are able to make.

Before you continue reading, it might be time for you to make a decision. Simply reading this book is not enough. You have to decide to make changes in how you manage projects. Do not waste your time with this book unless you are ready to implement what it contains!

Imagine you could get advice from someone with over $2 billion worth of project experience. Would it be worthwhile to you to listen to someone who has worked with hundreds of thousands of project managers? Imagine what valuable secrets you could learn from one of the world's authorities on project management! If you think such guidance would be beneficial, then you are in the right place, reading the right book.

Project managers have no time to waste, and this book will not waste your time. Expect it to be to the point and not to contain a lot of fluff. Also expect to have to do a lot of thinking. Be prepared to make notes about what you will do differently as a result of reading this book.

Make your decision now! Do you have the guts to be a better project manager?

Before you begin, take time to write down the things that drive you crazy about projects; the problems that you commonly see on projects. Don't skip this or any other exercise, because all the exercises are designed for your benefit. Take the time to think things through.

Exercise:

What problems on projects drive you crazy?

Let's think about problems on projects. As you go through this book, look for ways to prevent or deal with those problems you just wrote down. That way you'll get more out of the book. But first, a word about prevention. Good project management doesn't only deal with problems, it focuses on preventing them. And studies show that the cost of dealing with problems could be as much as 100 times more than the cost of preventing them. The tools of project management are designed to prevent problems. Look for them as you go through this book.

As you read this book, I encourage you to take advantage of the additional features we have included to make your learning more fun.

Interactive Web-Based Content

You will love this! RMC has created a special Web site, (www. rmcproject.com/crash), specifically for readers of this book. Throughout the text, you will be invited to share your ideas and experience on a number of project management topics with other readers of this book. On the Web site, you will also have access to printable templates of forms used in this book, and additional tips, tricks and articles relating to topics discussed here.

Key Terms

Throughout this book, you will see sidebars containing important definitions to remember.

TRICKS OF THE TRADE® Tricks of the Trade

This book will teach you many tricks of the best project managers, indicated by our Tricks of the Trade® icon.

IN THE FIELD Applying It in the Field

This icon indicates stories contributed by real project managers. Learn the tricks they have created to make a difference on their real-world projects.

We would love to hear from you too. Watch our Web site, www.rmcproject.com for our annual Tricks of the Trade® contest. Send us your best trick, and maybe your story will appear in the next edition of this book!

Exercises

This book contains exercises for you to complete. Yes, you should write in the book in order to get the most out of it, and yes, the exercises are important. They will help you determine what you know and do not know, and what you might need to spend more time focusing on. I encourage you to complete all the exercises.

At the end of each chapter, you will find the following topics:

Throughout the Project

Many of the concepts introduced in this book are first used during the early stages of a project; in initiating or planning. However, they are utilized throughout the project. This section of each chapter will walk you through the application of the concepts throughout the project.

Team Members

Project management activities are not done by just the project manager, they are done with the help of team members. Therefore, each chapter includes a section about how team members should be involved. This section has an added benefit. Reading it will give you a better understanding of the topics presented in the chapter.

Chapter Summary
Key Concepts
A summary of key concepts at the end of each chapter will help you solidify in your mind what you have learned.

Questions for Discussion
Considering these questions will take you from the context of this book and into the real world, making sure you understand the content well enough to make that transition. These questions are also used in universities and college courses designed to make use of this book.

Action Plan
At the end of each chapter you will be asked to think about what you have learned in that chapter and how you will apply that knowledge to your real-world project management efforts. Don't ignore this important idea. You will see immediate rewards as you apply what you have learned.

Exercise:

TRICKS OF THE TRADE: No matter how much training or experience you have managing projects, it's important to realize that you've got a lot of good ideas. Tricks are important. Tricks for managing and getting things done. I'd like you to think about what your tricks are. Start now by making a list of YOUR tricks. Add to them as you read. See how many more you will add by the end of this book. Imagine the difference the new tricks will make on your projects!

My Tricks for Managing Projects

The first thing you need to understand about project management is that it is proactive. Let me tell you a story.

A project manager was telling a group of people about a "great success" he recently had on his project. The project was the installation of a major telecommunications system. "You should have seen my team on this project! When the two major pieces of equipment needed for this system were delivered, we discovered there was no place to store them until they were installed. Instead of having a nine-day delay from returning the equipment and having it redelivered when we were ready, we were able to find a place to store the equipment nearby after only two days of searching!"

Let's stop and think about this story for a second. (Here it is time to decide if you are going to read AND do the exercises; are you really ready to change?)

Project Management

A systematic process used to initiate, plan, execute, control, and close a project to meet defined objectives

A science and an art

Exercise:

How would you feel if you were this project manager?
Would you feel on top of the world? Would you feel you deserve a raise or promotion?

Was the project successful? Why or why not?

Answer:

If you thought you would feel great and should get a raise or a
promotion, then you missed something important. The project
manager should have been fired, not promoted. Look at the story
again. See something you missed the first time?

You should ask, "Why did he not realize he needed a place to put
the equipment?" The project manager certainly worked miracles,
but he focused his expertise on dealing with the problem, rather than
preventing it!

How did you do on this exercise? Did you get the point? If so, then I
can see you becoming an even greater project manager.

Don't get started in project management by making the mistakes
other project managers do. A project manager's job is not to deal with
problems, but to prevent them.

Project Management Is Both a Science and an Art

Many inexperienced project managers rely on the art piece of project
management, which is often just their ability to manage or get along
with people. Why would we need a science?

The Science of Project Management
If you think of projects
from a company perspective, projects cost companies and other
organizations time and resources, and could negatively affect their
reputations. Just think of any company you have recently heard about
in your local news. Was the negative publicity related to a project?
Think about the increasing amount of change and the increasing
amount of competition in the marketplace today. You can see how

something needs to be done to help get work done faster, cheaper, and easier.

What about the personal perspective? Are you overloaded with projects right now? Do you KNOW you will be successful on each one? Do you even know how success is defined for each one? Do you have a plan for managing each one?

From both a company and a personal perspective, the science of project management is needed. To put it plainly, let's imagine a project manager needs to move a lot of baggage from one place to another. She tries a sled, and then she tries a cart with square wheels, and finally she invents a round wheel. She gets into town, only to discover that everyone else already is using a round wheel invented by someone thousands of years ago, and the wheel design and materials have vastly improved since then. Most project managers reinvent the wheel, not realizing there is already a science of project management in existence, and all they need to do is adapt it to their projects and their organizations.

So what is the science of project management? There are many answers, but basically it includes an accepted step-by-step process for managing a project.

Real project management is a systematic process of initiating, planning, executing, controlling, and closing a project. Note the phrase "systematic process." Do you have a step-by-step process? You should have one to be successful. Project management does not mean "wing it."

Let me help you take huge steps forward in understanding project management by providing you with an overall process. Such a real-world process is outlined in the following table. It applies to both large and small projects. For smaller projects, each step might take only a few minutes. For larger ones, each step might take a few days.

Rita's Process Chart

Initiating	Planning	Executing	Monitoring & Controlling	Closing
Select project manager	Determine how you will do planning—part of management plans	Acquire final team	Measure against the performance measurement baselines	Develop closure procedures
Determine company culture and existing systems	Create project scope statement	Execute the PM plan		Complete contract closure
		Work to produce product scope	Measure according to the management plans	
Collect processes, procedures and historical information	Determine team	Recommend changes and corrective actions		Confirm work is done to requirements
	Create WBS and WBS dictionary		Determine variances and if they warrant corrective action or a change	
	Create activity list	Send and receive information		Gain formal acceptance of the product
	Create network diagram			
Divide large projects into phases	Estimate resource requirements	Implement approved changes, defect repair, preventive and corrective actions	Scope verification	Final performance reporting
	Estimate time and cost		Configuration management	
Identify stakeholders	Determine critical path	Continuous improvement		Index and archive records
	Develop schedule		Recommend changes, defect repair, preventive and corrective actions	
	Develop budget	Follow processes		Update lessons learned knowledge base
Document business need	Determine quality standards, processes and metrics	Team building		
		Give recognition and rewards	Integrated change control	
Determine project objectives	Determine roles and responsibilities	Hold progress meetings		Hand off completed product
			Approve changes, defect repair, preventive and corrective actions	
Document assumptions and constraints	Determine communications requirements	Use work authorization system		Release resources
	Risk identification, qualitative and quantitative risk analysis and response planning	Request seller responses	Risk audits	
Develop project charter		Select sellers	Manage reserves	
	Iterations—go back		Use issue logs	
Develop preliminary project scope statement	Determine what to purchase		Facilitate conflict resolution	
	Prepare procurement documents		Measure team member performance	
	Finalize the "how to execute and control" aspects of all management plans		Report on performance	
	Create process improvement plan		Create forecasts	
	Develop final PM plan and performance measurement baselines		Administer contracts	
	Gain formal approval for plan			
	Hold kickoff meeting			

As you review the table, ask yourself, "How much of what is listed here do I know? How much do I do? What do I still need to understand?"

Be careful—such a process is NOT a process for doing the work (e.g., design, code, test; correctly called the project life cycle), but rather a step-by-step process for managing projects (a project management process).

It is important for you to understand the primary focus of each of the project management processes. We will not cover the details of each of them here. Remember that the big things that will make the most improvements on your projects are described in this book.

Initiating The first step in project management is initiating. What do we need before we even start planning the project? Think of initiating as trying to tie a rope around the project, figuring out what its limitations are, what we are being asked to do. Then initiating will make a lot more sense to you. We can't just take a magic wand and hope it's all going to come out in the end. We want to get everyone on the same page. We need clear communication from our management, and from our sponsor, as to what it is they want us to do. We also must identify any constraints and limitations. That's the idea behind initiating. The result of this process is an approved project charter, which will guide the rest of the project.

Planning Imagine you got a chance to do something twice. Would it be better the second time? This is what project planning is about. There is a lot of time spent planning; walking through the project so when you start to actually implement the activities to complete the project, they go quickly and smoothly. Everyone knows what they're doing. In some industries, planning could take 60 percent of the length of the project time!

The focus of planning is to save project time and money, and to

Project Life Cycle

What do you need to do to DO the work (e.g., designing, coding, testing, etc.)

Project Management Process

What you need to do to MANAGE the work (initiating, planning, executing and controlling, closing)

Project Management Plan

A document containing all the results of the project planning efforts

A detailed plan for accomplishing the project charter and project scope statement

It may change over time, but it is intended for use as a day-to-day management tool

improve your reputation. If you keep this in mind, you'll be more apt to follow through with what you learn here. It's also important to keep in mind that planning is going to help determine whether you can be successful. Planning is a key element of project management. Walk through the project before you do it. Planning culminates in the creation of a project management plan; a plan for the whole project. It contains the results of all the work shown in the planning column of Rita's Process Chart on page 12.

Executing and Controlling
This is the time to put the project management plan into action. The project manager has two functions: execute, which is to assist or help, and control, which means to measure. Be sure the work gets done according to the plan. Be sure end dates and budgets are met. Focus on completing the plan. Just get it done!

Closing
This is the chance for you, the project manager, to show just how good you are. Tie up all the loose ends. Make sure everything is finished. Make sure you have met the sponsor's, customer's, and stakeholders' needs. Prove you were successful, in some kind of final report. Determine what information from this project you might use to help make your next project easier. Throw a party to celebrate your project's success.

Follow the Whole Process
Want to save real time in the real world? Many project managers jump into a project (or are thrown in) when the work has already started. Initiating and planning MUST be done for all projects. Project management does not add time; it just moves time from when the work is being done (executing and controlling) to planning. Project management focuses on preventing problems, therefore, the work described as part of initiating and planning is not optional. Initiating and planning activities prevent problems later and SAVE time. They should be done even if a project has already started. It is essential to go back to those activities if you are assigned to manage a project that is already in progress.

The "Triple Constraint" A project manager needs to manage all aspects of the project, not only time and cost. One aspect of the project can affect all the others. These aspects are known as the "triple constraint" (even though there are six aspects), as illustrated below.

"Triple Constraint"

Time, Cost, Scope, Quality, Risk, Customer Satisfaction

Aspects of a project that the project manager must keep in balance based on identified priorities

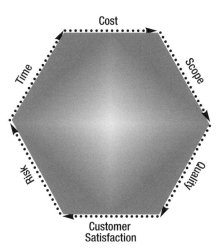

It is the responsibility of the project manager to integrate all aspects of the project, pulling them together in order to produce a successful result.

Another important point to remember is that project management is iterative. That is to say, as a project progresses, the proactive project manager may wish to repeat many of the previous steps as more and better information about the project is uncovered.

The Art of Project Management Since we have talked about the science of project management, how about the art? The art of project management is really about HOW project managers use the science of project management. How do they acquire realistic estimates from those who will do the work? How do they ensure the schedule is really agreed to and bought into by everyone? The art of project management should center on HOW the science is used, not just people skills.

The art of project management includes skills such as:

- Influencing the organization to get things done
- Taking risks
- Being innovative, thinking outside the box
- Setting performance standards
- Organizing the project, processes, and people
- Clarifying issues and objectives
- Planning for the future, strategizing
- Prioritizing issues and alternatives
- Solving the "real" problems
- Being oriented to the big picture
- Driving toward achieving objectives
- Managing relationships with everyone
- Resolving conflicts
- Negotiating
- Knowing what and how to communicate
- Managing communications
- Delegating
- Building the team
- Rewarding performance
- Leading so people follow
- Giving feedback
- Being politically aware
- Having financial know-how
- Walking on water
- Not having to be the technical expert—that role falls to the team members

Team Members

Team members' role in the project management process is explained throughout this book. In general, it is important to realize that everyone has projects and that a basic skill set of all those who are involved with projects is to be trained in project management. Therefore, the team should:

- Understand the project management process
- Know what their role is in each step of the project management process
- Make sure they have clear assignments of work, plus clear assignments of any reporting, meetings, or other activities to be required of them on the project
- Push back when they feel the need
- Be the technical experts, provide technical advice

The art of project management also requires knowing the appropriate role of team members, including:

- Be willing to:
  - Tell the truth
  - Ask for help
  - Contribute ideas
  - Take responsibility
  - Be accountable
- Work toward the objectives of the project
- Be empowered: Participate in learning what needs to be done, when, and how their pieces fit into the project
- Find better ways to meet the project objectives
- Realize their work impacts other team members and the success of the project

Chapter Summary

Key Concepts

Project management:
- Is proactive
- Is a science and an art
- Is a systematic process
- Involves balancing all components of the "triple constraint"

Questions for Discussion

What is included in the "science" of project management?

What is included in the "art" of project management?

Why is it important for a project manager to focus on preventing problems, rather than dealing with them?

Action Plan

What will you do differently in your real-world project management
as a result of reading this chapter?

Imagine that your manager asks you to start walking. You ask, "Where do you want me to walk?" and she says, "I don't know; start walking now, and I will tell you where I want you to go in one hour." Would this be efficient? Would there be a strong probability that you would pick the correct direction in which to walk?

Here is another scenario. Imagine that you have a lot to do when your manager assigns you an additional project. After a few weeks of work, you discover that the project does not have the support of upper management and will likely be cancelled. How frustrating to waste your efforts! In some companies, this is a common occurrence. How can you gain support and cooperation for projects in an environment where projects are often cancelled? In such environments, team members often acquire the skill of delaying until the project is cancelled.

These two stories illustrate the value of the project charter; making sure the project is authorized and that everyone is on the same page. How valuable would that be? How much time and money could be saved?

Recently, I was working with a team of 16 people to help them improve their project management. I started off by asking them, "What is your project?" This team had been working on the project for six months, yet I received 17 different answers from 16 people. (One said, "It is either this or that!") Can you afford to have this happen? A project charter prevents this and many other problems from occurring. This is the reason a project charter is so important.

What Is Included in the Project Charter?

The project charter is a document issued by the project's sponsor that authorizes the project and the project manager.

> **Project Charter**
>
> A formal document issued by the sponsor that authorizes the project and the project manager
>
> It provides the high-level requirements for the project

Think of the project charter as a target, as something that will keep everyone focused throughout the life of the project. The project needs to be planned to reach this target. With that in mind, you can see that the contents of a charter should provide the basis for planning. So, what do you think should be included? The project charter includes:

Project Title and Description (Briefly describe the project.) A simple, high level description of what is the project.

Project Manager Assigned and Authority Level (The name of the project manager, and whether he or she can determine budget, schedule, staffing, etc.) This gives the project manager authority to make use of company resources to complete the project and may be a big help on projects when authority must be used to gain cooperation.

Business Need (Why is the project being done?) The project manager needs to know this, as he or she will need to make many day-to-day decisions keeping that business need in mind.

Project Justification (On what financial or other basis can we justify doing this project?) This can provide the project manager with a measure of success if the justification proves valid.

Resources Pre-assigned (How many or what resources will be provided?) Some projects come with a limited number of human resources available or with some team members pre-assigned. Others need office space, computers, etc.

Stakeholders (Who will affect, or be affected by, the project (influence the project) as known to date?) This is the sponsor's impression as to who are the stakeholders. Stakeholder analysis comes later in the project management process.

Stakeholder Requirements as Known (What are the requirements related to both project and product scope?) These are the requirements that have been used to justify the project. Further work to clarify and finalize requirements will come later.

Product Description/Deliverables (What specific product deliverables are wanted, and what will be the end result of the project?) A measure of project success is that all the deliverables are met. It is important to have a clear picture of what constitutes the end of the project and what is the end result. Is it a report or a design? Should the design be tested, or just created?

Constraints and Assumptions (Are there any limiting factors? Is anything assumed to be true that may not be true?) Constraints can be cost-related (complete the project for no more than $100,000) or time-related (complete the project by May 1st). Assumptions need to be reviewed throughout the project, since an assumption that is proven not to be true will cause changes in scope and other parts of the project management plan.

Signed and Approved By: _____
Senior Management/Sponsor(s)

The charter requires a signature(s) in order to give authority and make the project official. Depending on the environment in which your project will be completed, there could be more than one signature on the project charter.

Do not underestimate the value of the project charter! The project charter is such an important document that a project cannot be started without one. If the project charter is your target for the project and serves as a definition of how success will be measured, then without a project charter, the project and project manager cannot be successful!

A project charter provides, at a minimum, the following benefits:

- Formally recognizes (authorizes) the existence of the project, or establishes the project—this means a project does not exist without a project charter
- Gives the project manager authority to spend money and commit resources
- Provides the high-level requirements for the project
- Links the project to the ongoing work of the organization

If the above is not enough to convince you, how about this list of reasons to have a charter?

- To make sure you understand the sponsor's needs
- To provide key information needed to get started
- To provide a mechanism to make sure everyone is on the same page later in the project
- To provide a basis to plan the project
- To make sure the sponsor's needs are not forgotten later in the project
- To protect the project manager by having a description of what he or she is being asked to accomplish

The project charter is also:

- Issued by a sponsor, not the project manager or the project team
- Created during initiating
- Broad enough so it does not NEED to change as the project changes

TRICKS OF THE TRADE® When we are starting project management, it can be difficult to get others, such as the project sponsor, to fulfill their roles. They may never have learned project management, or may not understand what their role in the process should be. To deal with this problem, the project manager has the following options.

- Do not do the project. If you cannot get a charter, either the project is not determined, the scope is unsure, or there is no support for the project. In any case, it would be wasteful to start a project under these circumstances.

- Complete the charter yourself by asking management questions related to the content of the charter. Fill out the charter as you discuss the questions, and have management sign it right then.

- Create the charter yourself. Publish it all over, and provide copies to all team members, stakeholders, and team members' bosses in order to cast it in stone.

Exercise:
What's Wrong with This Picture?

Using what you have learned in this chapter, analyze this sample project charter.

Project Charter
Project Title:
Build a house
Project Manager Assigned:
ABC Homebuilder
Goal:
To complete the house in 90 days
Business Case:
This newly married couple wants a new home built for them in a Chicagoland suburb
Product Description:
2 story vinyl-sided home with 3 bedrooms and 2 bathrooms on a ¼ acre lot
Signed and Approved By:
_____
Storm and Wendy Weather (future homeowners)

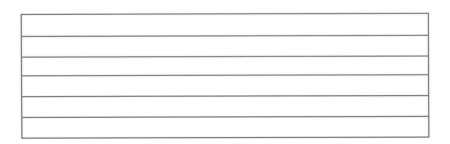

Answer:

- The charter has a title, but no detailed project description.
- The project manager is assigned, but what exactly is ABC Homebuilder going to do on this project?
- The goal is to complete the house in 90 days, but what happens if the 90 days are in the winter? How will freezing temperatures affect this project?
- Are there any assumptions or constraints?
- Does this couple have financing? Do they have another home to sell in order to move and pay for this home?
- This product description does not give the exact location of the home or enough detail to know what is and is not going to be included in the house. What are the deliverables? What are the due dates for the deliverables?
- Storm and Wendy are one of the sponsors, but if they are planning to get a mortgage for the home, the mortgage company would also be a sponsor.

Exercise:

Create a project charter for your real-world project.

Project Charter				
Project Title		**Project Manager**		
Project Description				
Project Manager Authority Level	Can the Project Manager determine budget, schedule, staffing, etc.?			
Business Need	Why is the project being done?			
Project Justification				
Resources Preassigned				
Stakeholders	Role	Impact	Influence	Risk Tolerance
		Options are: 4: High 3: Medium 2: Low-medium 1: Low	Options are: 4: High 3: Medium 2: Low-medium 1: Low	
Stakeholders' Requirements Related to Both Project and Product Scope				
Product Description	Describe the features & functions of the product of the project	Not in this Project		
Deliverables	List the customer deliverables below	Due date		
Prioritized Constraints	Scope - List Priority(ies)			
	Time:	Cost:		
	Quality:	Risk:		
	Customer Satisfaction:	Scope:		
Sponsor Signature	Signature			
	Printed Name			
	Date			
Project Manager Signature	Signature			
	Printed Name			
	Date			

Scope Creep

Uncontrolled changes
that add new work
or new features to
an already approved
project

Throughout the Project

The planning process will determine if the project can be completed within the confines of the project charter. Any changes to the project charter must be approved by the signer of the project charter. Any change to the project charter can affect the entire plan for completing the project (e.g., the cost, schedule, and risk for the project) and should be considered a huge change to the project.

During the life of the project, stakeholders can easily lose track of what the project is trying to accomplish. Here are some tricks, using the project charter, to prevent this from happening.

TRICKS OF THE TRADE: The project manager can use the project charter to remind everyone involved on the project exactly what the project is. It is a great help in preventing or limiting scope creep.

TRICKS OF THE TRADE: Have the project charter graphically designed (so it looks official). Then send color copies to all stakeholders and team members' bosses to post on their walls. This keeps the focus on what is the project, and therefore what is not in the project (thereby preventing some scope creep). It will also keep team members reminded of the project, making them more apt to complete their work assignments.

TRICKS OF THE TRADE: Design the approved project charter to be used as a screen saver by all team members throughout the project. This keeps the project in the minds of the team members, and serves as a visible reminder to all who see it that an important project is underway.

TRICKS OF THE TRADE: Review the charter with the team members at team meetings one third and two thirds of the way through the project in order to keep them focused on the project. Not only will this prevent some scope creep, it will also help the team see if they are off track.

Team Members

Team members' role in the project charter can include:

- Review the project charter when they are assigned to the project
- Provide feedback on the project charter
- Make sure all the work they do falls within the project charter
- Evaluate any requested changes to make sure they fall within the project charter
- Reread the project charter during the project to keep it in focus
- Provide a copy of the project charter to their managers

Chapter Summary

Key Concepts

The project charter:
- Is a high-level target for the project
- Authorizes the project and the project manager
- Must be approved before project work is begun

Questions for Discussion

Why should a project manager NOT begin a project without an approved project charter?

How can the project charter be used during completion of project work?

© 2006 Rita Mulcahy • (952)846-4484 • info@rmcproject.com • www.rmcproject.com

Action Plan

What will you do differently in your real-world project management as a result of reading this chapter?

Imagine the following situation. Your boss walks into your office and says, "The system is not functioning properly. I am giving you a project to find out what is wrong and fix it. I need the work done by June 25th, and I can assign you only four people from our company to help." Is this a project?

Think again. Many aspects of this story may be familiar to you, but does the situation describe a project?

What Is a Project?

A project has a beginning and an end. The desired result is known and clearly defined at the beginning, before work on the project is started (e.g., this project will be completed when the system is working up to the performance level achieved prior to the problem). Though an end was not described in the "Figure out what is wrong and fix it" situation, one can see that asking a question might clear up what is the end, and may result in the response as shown above. So, is this a project? Please read on.

Another characteristic of a project is that it can be organized to the point of being able to commit to an end date and/or an end budget. Would you be willing to stake your reputation on being able to complete this project on time? If your answer is, "I always have this situation thrown at me," then perhaps you have been missing something important. In fact, almost 90 percent of the project managers I come in contact with also miss this. The answer to my question is that it is not just one project. It is at least two projects!

Each project needs to be staffed and scheduled and an end date or time needs to be agreed to. In the situation described, you cannot estimate or schedule "fix it" until you know what is wrong with it. Therefore, this is at least two projects, "Figure out what is wrong" and "Fix it." Get it?

Project
Work which creates a unique product, service, or result
It has a beginning and an end
It has interrelated activities

For every "project" supplied by management, the customer, or any other source, the project manager must look at the assignment and break it down into appropriate projects that can be planned, managed, and controlled. The project manager and the team can then believe they will be successful in completing the project, which has end dates and budgets that the team believes can be met. Breaking the work down to manageable projects helps to properly plan each project.

Exercise:

Apply what you have learned by trying these examples. How would you break the following work into projects?

Work	Potential Projects
Determine if a new enterprise computer application could be created and then create it	
Improve an existing product	
Create a new bridge for a growing community	

Answer:

Okay, did you go right to the answer? Why not try the exercise before looking at the answer?

Work	Potential Projects
Determine if a new enterprise computer application could be created and then create it	• Analyze requirements • Design the new computer program • Create the new program • Test the new program
Improve an existing product	• Determine why the old product needs improving and suggest improvements • Study the feasibility of various product improvements and determine which improvements will be done • Implement the improvements • Field test the improved product • Roll out the improved product
Create a new bridge for a growing community	• Analyze the impact on the environment • Develop detailed designs and contracts • Acquire the land needed for right of way • Advertise the project and select vendor(s) • Do the construction

Did you think that the bullets provided were parts of one project, rather than the titles for many projects? On small projects they could be. To be successful on large projects, the work must be organized into pieces or projects that can be completely planned with a realistic and agreed-upon schedule and budget. The "projects" on the left side of the table cannot meet these requirements, while the projects listed on the right side can.

Program

A group of interrelated projects managed in a coordinated way

TRICKS OF THE TRADE To determine how many projects you really have, consider the following questions:

- Does the work have a defined beginning and end?
- Can you feel confident in your end date and end budget for the project to the point of staking your reputation on them?
- Will you use substantially the same resources for completing all the work?
- Do all parts of the work have the same focus and the same primary deliverables?

If you said no to any of these questions, you have more than one project.

What Is a Successful Project?
Completing all the work of the project:

- On time
- Within budget
- With an acceptable quality level
- With an acceptable risk level
- With stakeholder satisfaction

What is a Program?
A project that is too large or too long cannot easily be managed. It might be better to break it down into subprojects, or to call the "project" a program with many projects. A program is a group of interrelated projects managed in a coordinated way. The projects can be managed together as a program, or they can be planned and managed separately. To make a large project smaller, phases (feasibility, design, code, test, implement, turnover, etc.) could be planned and managed individually, making each phase of the project life cycle a separate project. Such actions make it easier to manage and control the project, thus increasing the probability of success.

Team Members

Managers, as well as team members, should have training in project management. When this is the case, it might be management or the sponsor that breaks the program into acceptable projects, rather than the project manager. Trained team members might also look for this problem and see the project from a perspective different than the project manager's. Therefore they may suggest that the project needs to broken down into projects further than what has already been done.

Chapter Summary

Key Concepts

A project:
- Is temporary and unique
- Has an agreed-upon end date and budget
- Has one focus

A program:
- Is a group of interrelated projects

Questions for Discussion

What are the advantages of breaking a large project into several
related projects (a program)?

How can you tell if your "project" is really more than one project?

Action Plan

What will you do differently in your real-world project management
as a result of reading this chapter?

Gaining, Creating, and Using Historical Information

Whenever we get a new project, there is a tendency to want to start the work immediately. The best project managers know better than to do this! Instead, they follow a good project management process. Such a process begins with the collection of all the data the team will need to effectively manage the project.

Historical Information

Records from past projects, used to plan and manage future projects, thereby improving the process of project management

Remember the previous discussion about reinventing the wheel? Here is a project management-specific example. A project manager was completing the design of a new building complex for a customer the company had worked with before. When the design was almost completed, the customer began requesting major changes. After four such changes, the project manager complained to another project manager about the changes. The other project manager replied, "That customer always waits until the end of the project before telling you what they really want."

Why didn't the project manager know about, and do something to deal with, this propensity of the customer? Could it be that he did what most project managers do, just start right in working on the project when it was assigned to him? It is unlikely the project manager looked for any historical information, or he would have discovered the propensity of the customer before he had to deal with it himself.

Imagine I was your boss, and I walked into your office to assign you a project. What would you do first? The answer is not to start the work; the answer is to find all the historical information available. Such historical information is valuable—like gold!—to the project manager.

Exercise:

Let's see how you do! Describe the type of information you need to collect before beginning a project.

Students often respond:

- What is wanted
- End date
- Cost objectives
- Resources available
- Reports needed

Can you see anything missing?

Here is a hint. We are looking for any information, including information from past projects, which the team can use to manage the current project.

Answer:

- Business need
- What the project is being asked to do
- How the project fits into or supports the company's strategic plan
- Who are likely to be stakeholders
- Contracts, if the work is done under contract
- Industry standards
- Government standards
- Minimum wage standards
- Construction standards
- Local and national government regulations

- How the company does business; defined processes and procedures
- Past relationships with the sponsor of the project, likely stakeholders, and team members
- What is going on in the company today
  - Other major projects
  - Their potential impact on this project
- The company's culture
- The company's future
- A list of people who may be good team members
- Basic information from past projects including:
  - Templates
  - Work breakdown structures
  - Estimates for each work package in work breakdown structures
  - Lists of risks
  - Lessons learned documents
  - Project schedules

TRICKS OF THE TRADE The collection of historical information obviously depends on the project. The more important the project, or the more perceived risk in the project, the more time should be spent collecting this information. Once you get beyond the basics, great project managers might even collect information including:

- Past history with the customer
- Past history of the resources on the project
- Information about personal relationships between any of the stakeholders that could affect the project
- Stakeholder risk tolerances
- Data regarding how the company organizational structure has positively or negatively affected past projects
- Information about how past projects and their successes might affect the current project
- All e-mails and meeting minutes from before the project was approved, including from the customer
- Any articles written about similar projects in trade journals, professional magazines, or even local newspapers

- Technical and project management literature containing articles, ideas, problems and solutions related to the project type
- Technical drawings, specifications
- Organizational charts
- Resumes of potential team members
- Reports from the marketing or sales department
- A description of what kinds of decisions the project manager can make on the project
- A list of official or unofficial experts who can assist the project team with the customer in identifying scope or risks, managing the project, etc.
- Priority of this project compared to all others in the organization
- Information about relevant cultural issues and suggested protocol, documentation, language barriers and social customs
- Data about key players for the team and the customer:
    - What are their stated objectives?
    - What are their hidden objectives?
    - What are their areas of influence?
    - What are their weaknesses?
- Thoughts of the experts and boss on how to complete the project
- Thoughts of the experts and boss on potential problems or problem areas

Collecting historical data will decrease project problems, and your project will take less time to plan and manage. Don't reinvent the wheel!

Throughout the Project

Throughout the planning and executing of your project, you will uncover useful information, create new processes, and make discoveries that will not only improve your project, but could be useful to others. Document these items as they are learned. This information, as well as your project management plan, work breakdown structure, etc., can become historical information. When your project is completed, collect all those lessons you have been documenting, and archive your project records so that other projects within your organization can benefit from your experience. Doing this will not only help you, it will help other projects and the company.

IN THE FIELD *Contributed by: Lisa Harper, PMP*
                          Cleveland, OH

After holding several lessons learned sessions at the end of projects, and not getting the needed attendance or the needed feedback, I came up with the following tricks for my lessons learned sessions:

The first trick is to ensure a high-level executive attends the session. It is generally not difficult to get the commitment of the executive that benefited most from the project. Some executives will even offer to provide opening or closing comments during the session. This trick increased my participation to 100 percent. Plus, the executives really appreciate being invited.

The second trick is to create an assignment for the meeting. Provide instructions to the participants one to two weeks prior to the session. The assignment is to create a presentation. Give them the option to team up with someone. Provide a template that lists "what went right," "what we could have done differently," and "what I learned." The most important piece of the instructions is to tell them to have fun! This trick increased the quantity and quality of data collected for my lessons learned sessions. You should see some of the creative PowerPoint presentations the teams have come up with. This also gives individuals the opportunity to utilize their presenting skills that they might not otherwise get.

I have received so much positive feedback from these sessions that I made this a standard practice on all my projects.

> **Lessons Learned**
> What was done right, what was done wrong, and what would be done differently if the project could be redone

Team Members

Team members' role regarding historical information can include:

- Provide the project manager with any historical information to which the project manager may not have access
- Review historical information and make use of it on their parts of the project
- Continually look for historical information that may be of use to the project
- Collect data on the current project to be included as historical information

Chapter Summary

Key Concepts

Historical information:
- Includes records from past projects
- Helps avoid "reinventing the wheel"
- Helps avoid repeating past mistakes of other projects
- Is collected at the end of each project
- Is documented for use in future projects

Questions for Discussion

How does historical information benefit a project manager?

What are good sources of historical information?

Action Plan

What will you do differently in your real-world project management
as a result of reading this chapter?

The term "stakeholders" encompasses everyone involved with or affected by the project, plus those who can positively or negatively affect the project. Stakeholders on a project can be a project manager's best friends or worst enemies.

A project manager was planning the purchase of buses for a particular route between two towns. The project manager remembered that stakeholders include people who can affect or negatively impact the project. In looking at the project, she noticed that a politician from one of the towns was very vocal about anything to do with his town. The project manager thought it reasonable that this politician could either help the project or get in the way. Instead of waiting for the politician to get in the way, the project manager planned to involve him on the project in a positive way, by keeping him informed.

During a meeting with her manager to discuss the project management plan for the project, the manager said, "Why would you want to have meetings with this politician? He is not even involved in this project! Remove this work from the project!"

What do you think happened when the work to get the politician involved on the project was removed by the manager? The politician felt slighted that he was not involved and started to force changes to the project. In fact, many of those changes seemed valueless, such as changing the interior color of the buses and changing the seat component to include more plastic. The net effect of not including this stakeholder in project planning was over $75,000 of changes and wasted effort.

How many stakeholders have you forgotten on your projects?

Stakeholders

People and organizations involved in or impacted by the project

People and organizations that can positively or negatively impact the project

Stakeholders can include:

Sponsor Provides the funding, supports the project

Management

Project Management Office Centralizes management of projects, provides templates, lessons learned and other guidance, may help provide resources

Project manager The person responsible for the project

Functional managers

Team

Customers Provide the product scope, approve changes

End users

Public

Funding sources

Most project managers fail to identify and properly involve stakeholders on their projects. Instead, they seem to focus on making changes whenever they are asked, and complain about it on the side. How about you?

Level of Influence

The degree to which a stakeholder can positively or negatively affect the course of a project

---

Exercise:

Let's give you a chance to apply what you have learned about stakeholders with the following case study.

An old (legacy) system has been negatively impacting the performance of three projects within a company. The legacy system is used in the accounting department and the finance department to create reports for financial analysis that are critical for company business decisions. The negative impact on the three existing projects is estimated to be greater than the cost of replacing the legacy system; therefore, company management has approved a project to create a new system to replace the legacy system. All projects in this company are required to follow company project, quality, and risk management standards. Though we cannot provide specific names of stakeholders from this case study, can you estimate who the stakeholders might be?

Stakeholder (by name)	Level of Influence 1 to 10 (10 is highest)	What will make them satisfied? (What are their requirements and expectations?)

Answer:

The key to any stakeholder list is to make sure all of the right people are included. In this example, many people overlook the person who created the legacy system. What if he or she is still working with the company and does not want his or her work to be replaced? Could this person get in the way?

How about the departments whose standards the project must follow? They will need to ensure the standards are adhered to, and they should be looking for the project to provide any suggestions for improving the standards.

The case study says the legacy system was used to make critical company decisions. When identifying stakeholders, you might ask yourself, "What decisions?" "Who makes them?" and "What are they really using to make these decisions?" Why not ask those who use the data what they wish to see the new system provide while the "determine requirements" project is ongoing and before the "implement the requirements" project is started?

Key stakeholders almost everyone in my classes forgets are the project managers for the three other projects who have been negatively impacted by the legacy system. Wouldn't they have some insight into what the new system should and should not do? Couldn't they provide historical records of past problems with the old system? Wouldn't there need to be some interface between these projects? How many times have you forgotten the impact of other projects on yours in the real world?

The list of stakeholders would include:

- Creator of the legacy system
- Owners of company standards
- Those who will be using the system to make critical company decisions
- Project managers for the other projects
- Sponsor

- Team
- Project manager
- Project management office (if one exists)
- Management
- Accounting department
- Finance department

Was this hard? If so, this chapter will be of key importance to you. Not only is it important to determine early in the project who all the stakeholders are, by name, it is important to make sure you know how much they can influence your project, and what will make them satisfied.

Identify Each Stakeholder by Name

Why identify each stakeholder by name? The management of stakeholders is not general; it should be specific to the needs of the individuals involved. Some stakeholders will need to be involved in clarifying the project scope. Some stakeholders might have expectations that have not been put into requirements for the project, which will need to be discovered. Some stakeholders will need to be included in the project reporting cycle. Therefore, stakeholders need to be listed by name, rather than by department, whenever possible.

A great project manager, even a beginning one, knows that preventing problems is easier than dealing with them. The work of identifying stakeholders will pay off later in the project when the problems such as these occur less frequently:

- Added project changes and delays
- Missed requirements
- Added conflict
- Loss of expertise
- Rework
- Lower quality

Following are some tricks to help you with stakeholder identification.

When an entire department is really a stakeholder, a trick is to have one person from the department WIN the opportunity to represent the department on the project. Such work is worthy of being on a resume (curriculum vitae), and that stakeholder will participate more fully, having won the position.

 If identifying all the stakeholders is so important, how do you know if you have identified them all? Try this trick. Ask each stakeholder who they think the stakeholders are for the project. You are guaranteed to find more stakeholders.

 Here is another trick. Instead of asking, "Who are the stakeholders?" ask people who they think would most benefit from the project and who they think might be able to provide advice. Also, it is interesting to ask "Who does NOT want this project to succeed?" or "Who might get in the way of our completion of this project?" Just asking the question a different way can bring out different responses.

Estimate Each Stakeholder's Level of Influence

Each stakeholder will have some level of influence on a project, like the politician in the previous story. Somewhere during planning and managing a project, the project manager will have to juggle the needs of competing stakeholders. Knowing their influence levels will help handle this juggling.

Not all influence is related to job position. Have you ever seen someone with an administrative job title who can spread his or her influence around in order to get things done?

To determine influence, simply put a 1 to 10 rating next to each stakeholder's name. It does not have to be scientific. A guess will do.

 Asking team members to provide their understanding of each stakeholder's influence level will make the overall result more accurate. This may also generate discussions that could bring potential risks and project scope to light that had not previously been thought of.

What Will Satisfy Each Stakeholder?

What about satisfaction? Have you ever completed a project only to have the end product or service not used? How bad does that feel? No one likes to see this happen, yet it happens all the time in many industries. Ever ask yourself why?

Satisfaction is a very sophisticated thing to manage. What do you think is more important, measuring the "happiness" of stakeholders or making sure the project meets requirements? This is a hard question, but the best answer is both.

In addition to project requirements, stakeholders have expectations, which you must also uncover. These are things the stakeholders expect to happen to them, their department, or the company as a whole. These tend to be much more ambiguous than stated requirements, or they may be undefined requirements. They may be intentionally or unintentionally hidden.

Expectations include such things as, "I expect this project will not interrupt my department's work," or "I expect the system will be dramatically improved as a result of the project." Naturally, expectations that go unidentified will have huge impacts across all components of the "triple constraint." Expectations can be converted to requirements. A great project manager will make sure to identify all of the stakeholders' expectations.

We talked about who are stakeholders and how to identify them, but why bother? This process, as just described, requires a lot of work and a lot of thought! There is one overreaching reason it is worth the effort. As we saw in the bus project story earlier in this chapter, a stakeholder who is forgotten or ignored in the planning process will make changes later.

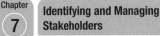
So, you might say, all projects have changes. That may be true. All changes are not necessarily bad, but they are expensive. Some studies show that a change made during project executing will cost 100 times more than a change made during planning the project. 100 times!

TRICKS OF THE TRADE Here is a revolutionary concept. If the team members are considered stakeholders, then shouldn't the project manager ask them what will make them satisfied?

Exercise:

Think of all the team members you have worked with, as well as your own experience as a team member. Then make a generic list of possible things team members would want as a result of working on a project.

Answer:

It is important to realize that many team members will do things to work toward something they consider positive, or to move away from something they consider negative. The following are a few of the items you might have included on your list.

- They want to be released from the project, as they have too much other work to do
- They want to work on the project because the product of the project will solve a problem they have
- They need an opportunity to grow their reputation in their own department
- They are bored with their current work and want to learn

something new
- They want to use their efforts on the project to gain a promotion
- They want to make sure they are able to leave work on time for the next three months because they have commitments in the evenings
- They do not mind working on the project unless it interferes with project X, the one they are really interested in

Now add your ideas to the list on our Web site (www.rmcproject.com/crash), and find more ideas you had not thought of.

Great project managers will keep these things in mind as they make decisions throughout the life of the project. They will influence the schedule, budget, how meetings are held, who is assigned what project scope and project management-related work, and much more.

TRICKS OF THE TRADE® Uncover communication preferences when identifying stakeholders.

Have you ever had someone say, "You never told me," when the topic had been mentioned in a report which that person did not read? How about the times you e-mailed someone about an important issue and they did not read it in time? Communication is one of the top problems on projects, but only because we do not manage it. The trick is to start thinking in the beginning of the project, when the stakeholders are first identified, about how people want to be communicated with.

Some stakeholders would prefer to be called, others prefer to be e-mailed, and some may just want a hard copy of a report. Communication on a project is a two-way street, and should therefore go from the project manager to the stakeholders and from the stakeholders to the project manager, throughout the life of the project. If the best way to communicate with each stakeholder is not identified, the project manager is simply adding communication problems to later parts of the project. Great project managers are proactive about communication. They understand how each stakeholder wants or needs to be communicated with BEFORE the project starts, and as each new stakeholder is identified throughout the life of the project.

Let's take the table we used in the previous exercise and add communication requirements to it. This column will include specific instructions for how to contact each stakeholder if needed.

Exercise:

Complete the following chart for your real-world project.

Stakeholder	Level of Influence	What will make them satisfied?	Communication Requirements

You will find many more tricks for effective communication later, in Chapter 12 of this book.

Throughout the Project

Stakeholders should be involved in planning the project and managing it more extensively than you might be doing on your projects. For example, stakeholders may be involved in the creation of the project charter and the preliminary and project scope statement.

Stakeholders may become risk response owners, and are also involved in:

- Finalizing requirements
- Project management plan development
- Approving project changes
- Scope verification
- Identifying constraints
- Other parts of risk management

Managing Stakeholders

Now you know who your stakeholders are, and you know what they want. What next? A project manager must continue to do the following regarding stakeholders:

- Identify any new stakeholders, and include their needs in the stakeholder list
- Make sure all stakeholders' needs are met, including those of the team, by including interactions with stakeholders in the project manager's management activities
- Create and use recognition and reward systems (See more on this later in this chapter)
- Keep track of stakeholders' issues and document their resolution

Identify New Stakeholders This seems simple, but it is often forgotten by project managers. Continue to use the tricks for identifying stakeholders while the work is being done. Remember that it is harder to identify stakeholders in the beginning of the project, and it is only while the project is being worked on that some stakeholders will be identified.

TRICKS OF THE TRADE® Look for new stakeholders every time there is a change requested on the project. This is often how new stakeholders get involved in the project.

TRICKS OF THE TRADE® Include an agenda item, "Who are the stakeholders?" at a team meeting partway through the project to help identify new stakeholders.

Make Sure All Stakeholders' Needs Are Met Stakeholders'

needs must continue to be met and their issues resolved throughout the project. In the heat of the battle to complete a project, many project managers drop their efforts to manage stakeholders. This usually leads to a decrease in the effectiveness of their project management. Forgetting the stakeholders later is a sign of an inexperienced project manager, focused on dealing with problems rather than fulfilling the main job of preventing problems.

The following are some tricks great project managers might use in managing stakeholders while the project is underway.

TRICKS OF THE TRADE: A project manager knows that some of the team members felt strongly that certain scope should have been part of the project. Anticipating that the team might continue pressing to get the scope added, the project manager communicates the following at the first team meeting. "During planning, there were a number of suggested pieces of scope that were specifically determined not to be a part of this project. I will be looking for any attempts to add them back into the project."

How about this situation?

TRICKS OF THE TRADE: During requirements gathering, a stakeholder expressed concern about how much of her staff's time would be needed on the project. While finalizing the project management plan, the project manager contacts her and says, "You know by now that some of your staff will be needed on this project. However, I understand your concern. I have designed our project's monthly report to clearly show you when and how much of your staff time will be needed. Will this help you manage your department and minimize the negative impact of this project on your department?"

Let's try another situation.

Exercise:

A project manager is working on a project with 14 stakeholders who need to be involved and kept updated on the project. As the project manager, what would you do to fulfill those needs?

Answer:

A beginning project manager would say, "Send them copies of the project reports." This is certainly a good general practice, but I am trying to help you become a more expert project manager. Let's go beyond this basic idea. How about the following tricks?

 Invite stakeholders to some team meetings so they feel they are a part of things and so they can see just how complex some project issues are.

 Send a special report geared just to the stakeholders, and include things that the stakeholders have done to help the project.

TRICKS OF THE TRADE. Have a meeting for all of the stakeholders so that they can be updated on the progress of the project and how it might affect them.

Add your best ideas to our Web site, (www.rmcproject.com/crash), and access the contributions of others.

Why bother doing such work? Such actions are proactive and make the stakeholders feel that their needs and concerns are being considered, even if they are not agreed to. These actions also serve the valuable function of keeping open communication channels with the stakeholders. They enable stakeholders to inform you of potential changes, added risks, and other information. Such actions therefore PREVENT problems later and catch problems before they become too large.

IN THE FIELD *Contributed by: Hajisaleh Kutchhi*
Pune, Maharashtra, India
This trick could be used for any long running maintenance project where resource movements are quite frequent. Problems in this type of project often include getting new resources trained as quickly as possible, and the lack of available documentation on application systems. New team members may spend hours looking for

information which is urgently needed, in order to fix a problem on the project.

This type of situation can be very well handled by creating a "knowledge repository" for the project. This knowledge repository has A-to-Z information about the project, for new team members to refer to. This knowledge repository thus reduces the effort of experienced/existing project staff towards training the new team members, and enables new team members to work on the various project activities independently.

In particular, the repository includes:

1. Induction and Training Program—Information for a new team member to study.
2. "Induction Checklist"—Items like completion of Induction course, important and "must know" information for the project, i.e., getting various access rights to various systems/functions, etc.
3. Log of issues and defects encountered on the project in the past (particularly frequent defects) and their resolutions and history of actions.
4. "How do I" documents—The processes to perform various project-specific routine tasks required as part of day-to-day activities. Possible examples include; "How do I promote code in so-and-so environment?" "How do I deploy the application?" "How do I set up a new batch job?" "How do I set up so-and-so data?" etc.
5. Contact List—A list of all contacts that may need to be reached for various reasons while working on the project. This may include DBAs, business users, technology staff, staff whose projects are dependent/related to this project, subject matter experts, module leads and managers, production support desk, and other useful help desk numbers.
6. Properly indexed and organized documentation on project domain.
7. Proper documentation on application systems of the project, transaction flows within the system, interface details and any other information which is useful and which is required frequently during the project.

8. Technical manuals which can be referenced when required.
9. Other items as per requirements of the project.

This knowledge repository can be maintained in any shared drive or in a configuration management tool like Microsoft Visual Source Safe, or it can be developed as a stand-alone Web application. Such a repository will make the life of every team member easier and will help in the smooth execution of the project.

What about functional managers, those people who "own" or manage resources (people) that are needed for the project? Have you ever gone to them to gain resources and found them uncooperative? If you have ever been in this situation, think again. Have you considered why that might be? Functional managers are not frequently compensated for their efforts to support projects. (Maybe they should be!) They have other work to do, and then the project manager comes to them and asks them to drop everything to help the project. The problem in this situation is not the functional manager, it is the project manager!

"What?" you might say. It is the project manager's responsibility to communicate to all stakeholders, including functional managers, the schedule for the project, in advance. Therefore, there should rarely be an instance when the project manager has to say, "I need resources NOW!" Any time a project manager does this, the individual is, in reality, communicating that he or she is not in control of the project. This is not a good thing for a project manager.

Managing stakeholders also includes managing team members. Not all teams are large, but even the smallest teams require management. Have you ever realized that the reputation of each of your team members is in your hands? How well the project goes will reflect on their careers. If a team member believes the project will be unsuccessful, he will remove himself from as much work on the project as possible so it does not tarnish his reputation.

The project manager has a duty to team members to make sure there is a realistic schedule so the team members can know when they need to complete work on the project. They need to be provided with a reward system. They need to be asked their opinions and to contribute to the development of the project management plan. They need to help control the project. Do you treat them as servants?

Recognition and Reward Systems
Ask yourself, when was the last time someone said "thank you" to you? How good does it feel to be thanked, and why doesn't it happen more often? Expressions of appreciation should not be random or nonexistent in project management, but rather planned into the project by the project manager.

Exercise:

What are the benefits of recognition and reward systems?

Answer:

First you should realize that it will make you, the project manager, feel good to give rewards. Isn't that a reason to do it in itself? Other benefits of using rewards include:

- Increasing cooperation from those who win and those who do not receive the recognition
- Showing that the project manager appreciates the team's or stakeholders' efforts
- Keeping the team and stakeholders focused on performing in ways that benefit the project
- Keeping everyone focused on what is important to the project

To create a recognition and reward system, ask yourself how you will motivate and reward not only the team, but also each team member individually (because of course you have already identified each one by name during planning). This requires learning what each of your team members and stakeholders want to get out of the project, on a professional and personal level. The project manager asking questions to gain such information is required, not optional.

TRICKS OF THE TRADE® The project manager takes his or her knowledge of the needs of the stakeholders and then creates a recognition and reward system. Such a system might include the following actions:

- Offer a prize to the stakeholder who makes the biggest contribution
- Say "thank you" regularly
- Award prizes such as Team Member of the Month recognition, or cash prizes for performance
- Recommend team members for raises or choice work assignments, even though such actions by the project manager may not be officially part of the team members' performance reviews
- Send notes to stakeholders' managers about great performances
- Plan milestone parties or other celebrations
- Acquire training for team members paid for from the project budget
- Adjust the project to assign people to requested activities or to remove them from disliked activities
- Work with management to have a team member removed from the project if requested, and if it is possible
- Assign a team member to work where he or she can gain more knowledge

IN THE FIELD *Contributed by: V. S. Srividhya*
Chennai, Tamil Nadu, India

Based on the core complexity of a project, I design a contest for the team at the planning stage. For example, if it is a testing project, I call it the "Project Tester Award." If it is a Web page designing

project, I call it the "Designer Award." I announce the rules for the
same and the objective in the project kickoff meeting. The metrics are
regularly tracked and I send out notes or make mention of it during
status meetings. This promotes healthy competition among the team
members and also increases productivity. At the close of the project,
when we celebrate our success, I invite important stakeholders and
the team to a party. At this venue, I announce the winner of the award.
Although there is a single award given, I bring mementos for each and
every team member. As they come forward to accept their mementos,
I recognize their contributions to the project. Generally everyone
loves this. It also serves to make people enthusiastic to work on my
next project.

 Contributed by: V. S. Srividhya
Chennai, Tamil Nadu, India

When a project team is assigned to me, I get a contact list with each
person's name, address, phone number, e-mail address, and their
birthday. As the project work progresses, I make it a point to cut
a cake for every team member's birthday in our "war room." One
person is named as "party planner" and he or she coordinates the
party celebrations.

This small but neat trick goes a long way in team building. It also
gives the team members a chance to let their hair down and enjoy.

Winning Trick
Contributed by: Jackie Labbé, BSc.BM, PMP
Vancouver, British Columbia, Canada

My trick proved quite effective for ensuring some critical studies
and documents were completed on time. Since development takes so
long in my field, when people are actually at the end there is a big
crunch to get all the required studies and documentation in. People
are usually tired by this point, and I needed everyone to maintain
focus and be energized.

I developed a Lizard Race—a giant sized poster, with pictures of

Issue Log

A record used to track
issues on the project,
their status, and their
resolution

lizards traced out—all leading to the END. A lizard represented
a study or document. I then gave each "owner" a rubber lizard
from the local toy store. When the "owners" completed their race
(meaning study and document approved), they got to go to the race
poster, and stick their lizard on it with a rubber band. Then, they ran
to my office to collect their reward: chocolate bars for their team!
It was fun watching everyone get excited as they participated and
watched the race unfold! I would often arrive at my office to find
someone waiting with lizard in hand, smiling from ear to ear.

Issue Log One of the key things stakeholders complain about is
that their needs are forgotten by the project manager. Often this is
more of a feeling than reality. Many project managers use issue logs
to keep track of things that need to be resolved or discussed. Issue
logs are also a key way to make stakeholders feel that their needs are
being taken care of.

Note that issues are not the same as risks. We will discuss risks in
more detail in Chapter 13 of this book.

An issue log might look like the following:

Issue #	Issue	Date Added	Raised By	Person Assigned	Resolution Due Date	Status	Date Resolved	Resolution

TRICKS OF THE TRADE Keep the issue log in a public place, or post it, so that all
stakeholders will know that their issues are going to be
addressed, even if the issues are not resolved to their satisfaction.
Many people will accept a decision of "no" if they believe their issue
has at least been considered.

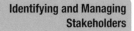
The stakeholder management process includes the following steps:

- Identify all the stakeholders by name
- Determine all of their requirements
- Rank the requirements by stakeholder
- Determine stakeholder expectations, and turn them into requirements
- Manage and influence the stakeholders' involvement
- Get them to sign off that the requirements are finalized
- Assess their knowledge and skills
- Analyze the project to make sure their needs will be met
- Let them know what requirements will and what requirements will not be met, and why
- Get and keep them involved in the project by assigning them project work, such as assisting with managing risk
- Keep their interests in mind
- Use them as expert advisors
- Make sure the project communicates to them what they need to know, when they need to know it
- Involve them, as necessary, in change management and approval
- Involve them in the creation of lessons learned
- Get their sign-off and formal acceptance during project closing

Team Members

Don't forget that team members are stakeholders too! Team members' role in identifying and managing stakeholders can include:

- Provide the project manager with their opinions on who are the stakeholders
- Constantly look for missed stakeholders
- Interview stakeholders to determine their expectations, as requested by the project manager
- Assist in managing the issue log

Chapter Summary

Key Concepts

When identifying stakeholders:

- Identify anyone who can affect the project or be affected by the project
- Ask the stakeholders "Who do you think are the stakeholders?" to discover any stakeholders you might have missed
- Determine stakeholder communications requirements and what will make them satisfied
- Continue to manage stakeholders, and identify new stakeholders throughout the project

Questions for Discussion

What are the dangers of failing to identify all stakeholders on a project?

During which part of a project should you attempt to identify stakeholders? Why?

What is the impact of an effective recognition and reward system on a project?

Action Plan

What you will do differently in your real-world project management as a result of reading this chapter?

Let's start off with an exercise.

Exercise:

What do you think the project manager's role is regarding scope? Could you put it in a sentence?

| |
| |
| |

Product Scope

Describes the product, service or result of the project

Many people say, "Complete the work asked of me," or "Manage all the scope changes as they arise." Neither of these should be the project manager's primary focus. It would be much more beneficial to the project manager's project, and to his or her career, to think of work relating to scope as, "Making sure all the scope that can be identified is identified in writing, and then managing the project to complete the scope and eliminate the need for unnecessary scope changes." Can you see the difference? The second phrase is more proactive and assertive, and manages the project in the best interest of the company. Real project management requires the project manager to know where the trouble spots are and to prevent them from hurting the project. Scope is certainly a potential trouble spot.

Project Scope

Describes the work needed to create a product, service or result (the product scope)

This definition of a project manager's work related to scope requires a new way of thinking for many project managers—scope must be completely identified before work starts! First let's think of why this is, and then think about how to make it happen in the real world.

Let me try an analogy. Imagine your project is to carry a small bag to a house 600 meters away. (Work with me here!) You start on your way, when all of a sudden someone adds large bag to your load. Then someone else adds two boxes. By this time, you realize that your plan to get to the house on foot is not effective, and you go back to get an automobile. The weather turns cold, and you also need to get a coat. The boxes are heavy, so you need more resources. See a pattern? The lesson here is that each time new scope is added, the ENTIRE project has to be replanned!

You have heard me say this before: Added scope might affect risk, cost, time, people, quality, and customer satisfaction, as well as other work already planned. The impact of all of these must be evaluated and the impacts minimized. For a project manager who understands this, there is no such thing as "Can't we just add this little piece of new work to the project?" Each change can affect the whole project.

There will always be some changes on the project, but unnecessary changes must be prevented and all changes must be evaluated, documented, and formally approved. Did you know there are tricks for avoiding unnecessary changes in the real world? The first step is to get complete requirements from your stakeholders.

Put yourself into the shoes of those that have requirements, or scope. In many cases, they would rather do anything than sit down and determine their requirements, especially if doing so requires them to reach consensus with others. It is often the wildest dream of busy people that a project manager could read their mind and just "make it happen." On many projects, those who have the requirements or scope do not understand the technical aspects of the project, nor what it would take to make their requirements happen. They want what they want, and they do not understand why getting it might be so difficult. The trick to obtaining complete scope requirements (or time or cost or any other requirements, for that matter) is to keep these thoughts and needs in mind. Here is an example of how you might do this. Pay special attention to the wording.

You might start by stating the following. "This is a challenging project because… so I can imagine the last thing you want to do is to clearly describe in writing all your requirements. However, you are very busy, and you want this project completed by a certain date. I estimate that the project will take up three times more of your time than it should if we do not get all the requirements now. In organizing the project, I will let you know if all the requirements can be completed by that date. But assuming they can, I will need to coordinate cost, people, quality, and technical issues in organizing this project." (Notice we do not say planning the project.) "I cannot effectively make use of these company resources if I do not have all the requirements. Can you take a minute to make sure you are providing me with all the requirements now, before it is too late?"

Depending on who you are talking to, you could be even more assertive by saying such things as, "I know that the last thing you want to do is sit down with the people in your department to finalize your needs. However, if we do not have all your requirements by May 12, I cannot promise that we will be able to accommodate your needs afterward." In other words, the best project managers will know this is a potential problem area. They will put the problem "on the table" and specifically address the stakeholders' dislike for completing their requirements.

Did you notice the statement made in the quote above, "Changes later will likely require more time?" Another important project management concept, as it relates to scope, is that scope equals cost and time. In other words, the project is planned to accomplish a defined scope for a certain cost or time. If the scope changes, the cost or time should also change!

Look again at the "triple constraint" graphic. Notice that all components must be balanced!

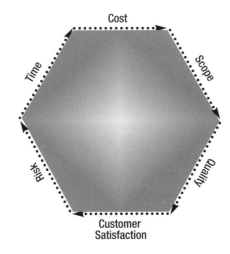

Keeping this scope management philosophy in mind, there needs to be a description of the scope, in writing, on all projects. Now you are really getting worried, aren't you? I have shown that one of the major problems you might already be experiencing, changing scope, is in part due to a lack of proper project management activity. Now I am adding flames to the fire by saying that requirements should be in writing. Let's look at why.

Communication is inherently flawed in many situations. If you add the international aspects of many projects and the multicultural aspects of almost all projects, communication can be even more of a problem. One area in which communication problems can be easily avoided relates to project requirements. The simple rule that requirements must be in writing forces people to be clear and more complete than they would otherwise be. Having requirements in writing also prevents miscommunication and allows the project manager to later say, "What you have asked for is not in the original requirements, and is therefore a change." Having requirements in writing will also help the project manager properly plan the project and all its components, and then prove success when the project is completed.

Let's summarize the important concepts presented so far.

© 2006 Rita Mulcahy • (952)846-4484 • info@rmcproject.com • www.rmcproject.com

- Scope must be as complete as possible before planning can start
- Scope must be in writing
- Planning requires integration of scope, time, cost, people, quality, and risk. Scope added later must also be evaluated for an impact to other aspects of the project
- Scope must be controlled
- Scope added after project work begins almost always causes a resulting schedule change

With all these important philosophical things described, let's go into detail. I hope you remember reading earlier in this book that there are two types of scope: product scope and project scope. Product scope describes the product of the project. It is usually created by the customer, or it is written from their point of view. The project scope is the description of the work needed to accomplish the product scope. Both are needed for a successful project. Both should be in writing. The product scope might describe performance requirements; the project scope describes how the project will accomplish them. The product scope might describe materials to be used; the project scope describes how those materials will be acquired.

On larger projects, there is often a preliminary project scope statement created before planning starts in order to obtain clear direction from management on the expected project scope. The preliminary project scope statement provides the project manager with the information needed in order to plan the project.

The preliminary scope statement varies by project and the project's needs. Think about what you would need to know about scope before you start to plan. Wouldn't you want more detail on the requirements, how success will be measured, and any information from the sponsor regarding risks, budgets, and schedules?

How do you know if you should create a preliminary project scope statement? Ask yourself:

Project Scope Statement

A document that describes the project deliverables and the work required to create those deliverables

Question	Yes or No
Is the project considered large in your organization?	
Does the project have major components that have never been done before within the company?	
Is the scope expected to change significantly as the project progresses?	
Is the team inexperienced in working on projects?	
Is the project a high priority project for the company?	

If you answered yes to three or more of the questions, it would be wise to have a preliminary project scope statement.

If there is a preliminary project scope statement, it is expanded in the planning process into the "final" project scope statement to be used on the project. This will include the entire description of the products or services to be provided by the project.

To complete the project scope statement, one might perform the following:

- Review what is and what is not included in the project
- Make sure all the stakeholders are identified and requirements are obtained from all of them
- Ask those who provided requirements how complete those requirements are
- Ask those who provided requirements who else might have requirements
- Make sure everyone knows that requirements must be finalized before planning can effectively start, and why this is true
- Make sure the stakeholders' needs, wants, and expectations are turned into requirements

© 2006 Rita Mulcahy • (952)846-4484 • info@rmcproject.com • www.rmcproject.com

What Is Included in the Project Scope Statement?

There are no templates for scope statements, as they differ based on the needs of the project. Many of the topics you might consider including are also addressed in the project charter. They are covered from a high-level perspective in the charter. The project scope statement addresses them in more detail.

Project Objectives Measurable success criteria

Product Scope Description Overall characteristics of the product of the project

Project Requirements Description of the product scope in detail

Project Boundaries What is and is not included in the project

Project Deliverables Product and project deliverables

Product Acceptance Criteria How will you know the products of the project are acceptable

Project Constraints Detailed time and cost and other factors that affect scope

Project Assumptions Detailed lists of what is assumed to be true that may not be true (e.g., the computers will work when turned on, no more than two other projects will be initiated while this project is ongoing)

Initial Project Organization Members of the team and how they will be organized

Initial Identified Risks (Note that more formal risk management comes later)

Schedule Milestones Including their imposed dates

Fund Limitations For the whole project or for any deliverables

Cost Estimate Plus its level of accuracy

Project Configuration Management Requirements The level of such control on the project

Project Specifications Identifies any such documents

Approval Requirements Who can approve what

Did you notice:

- How much detail can be included in the project scope statement
- How the rest of project planning will center around this important document
- That this could be one of the most important documents in project management
- That such a document could take time and coordination with stakeholders to complete

Exercise:
What's Wrong With This Picture?
Using what you have learned in this chapter, analyze this sample

Project Scope Statement
A two story vinyl-sided home with three bedrooms and two bathrooms will be built by ABC builders in 90 days. The home will have no basement. It will have a two car garage. The builder will supply basic landscaping which includes grass and a parkway tree. Homeowners can pick their colors for interior. Carpet will be grade level II. The walls will be painted flat white. The builder will supply a one year warranty on major defects to the home.

Answer:
A scope statement should contain enough detail for the project manager to know exactly what is included in the project and what is not included. Does this scope statement answer questions such as the following?

- What does "colors for interior" refer to?
- What is grade level II carpeting?
- Where will the carpeting be installed and where won't it be installed?
- What about other flooring needs?
- For the warranty, what does "major defects" refer to? What kind of defects will not be considered under warranty?

Exercise:

Create a project scope statement for your real-world project.

Throughout the Project

When completed, the project scope statement becomes the central focus to control scope changes. It will help you determine if changes are within the planned work of the project or not, and the magnitude of any requested changes. The project scope statement can also be used to remind stakeholders of what is approved scope. It provides a clear basis to describe scope changes when they occur.

TRICKS OF THE TRADE On long projects, smart project managers review the project scope statement with stakeholders on a regular basis throughout the project. The goal is to identify scope changes, or parts of the project scope that need clarification. Finding such issues early, rather than waiting for them to arise, will help decrease the cost and other impacts of changes.

IN THE FIELD *Contributed by: Miriam Morris*
Toronto, Ontario, Canada

When I am defining the success criteria of the project with the sponsor and the team, I always ask them, "How do we set ourselves up for success?" We agree to a short list of SMART criteria and measures, and I document them in a simple table with 3 columns:

- Criteria Description and Measures
- Accountability—The accountability shows the name of the person who is accountable for achieving the measures that are deemed successful.
- Evaluation Date—The evaluation date is the date when the success will be measured. This could be end of the project or few months later, when the actual benefits are realized.

I bring this table to the status meetings on a regular basis and remind the team of our agreement on what success looks like. I have found it keeps the team motivated and it gets us over hurdles when they arise. There is a great feeling of accomplishment when the success is evaluated at the end of the project and we can prove to ourselves that we have been successful. Those who took the accountability on their shoulders at the beginning get the glory... and they want to do it again for future projects.

 Contributed by: Srinivas Vadhri
Cupertino, CA

I use this trick once the scope and timelines are fully defined and "set in stone," during my weekly communications or for any executive-level presentation. At the bottom of any communication, I include the following statement: "Scope and timelines approved by all stakeholders on ##/##/2006" in a small font. This reminds people, especially project sponsors, that everything is set in stone, and that any changes need to be analyzed against the "triple constraint."

 Winning Trick
Contributed by: Jeffrey Carpenter, PMP
Portland, OR

We all know the importance of establishing a change control process with our client and internal team. A good project management team takes care to establish a change control board, define members and define a process for identifying changes, categorizing them as defects or enhancements, in scope or out of scope, and then processing change requests. The problem often arises in the execution of this change control process. A project manager may feel bad about "nickel and diming" the client for small changes, particularly at the beginning of the project, so it is common to agree to ad hoc small changes on the fly at no cost without using the formal CCB process.

The problems with this include the following:

- It starts to set a precedent for how changes will be managed
- Without documentation of the small, "no cost" changes, the client forgets that you accommodated these changes for them —e.g., your goodwill efforts are quickly forgotten
- Unintended consequences can bite you later on
- Little changes can lead to big variances over time

Early in the project, I like to identify some "no cost" small changes, or even a mock change, and run it through the CCB process at the first scheduled internal team and client meeting. This is a non-threatening way to practice the process and, if necessary, revise the process with the client so that it becomes something that is rehearsed and understood. After running through the process, I take time with the client to identify the benefits of the controlled approach to change, as well as scenarios of what could have happened if the formal process had not been used.

Some clients see change control as a negative process associated with more cost to them, and some projects see it as a process that slows down decision-making. Practicing the process up front to work out kinks, demonstrating its value, and getting stakeholders comfortable with using it will serve the project well in the long run!!

Team Members

Team members' role in the project scope statement can include:

- Provide feedback on the project scope statement when they are assigned to the team to make sure it is as complete as possible
- Make sure all the work they do falls within the project scope statement
- Help evaluate whether requested changes fall within the project scope statement
- Look for scope creep and gold plating in the work they do and in the project work they see

Chapter Summary

Key Concepts

- Product and project scope must be determined before project work begins
- Changes to scope also impact other aspects of the "triple constraint"
- A project scope statement helps reduce unnecessary changes on a project

Questions for Discussion

What can a proactive project manager do to prevent unnecessary scope changes on a project?

What is the difference between product scope and project scope?

Action Plan

What will you do differently in your real-world project management as a result of reading this chapter?

Let's start with a story. A team member was overwhelmed one day at work, and one of his colleagues said, "My goodness, you look like you're completely out of control." He said, "You know, I am, because I was just assigned a new project. I have no idea how I'm going to get all of this work done." The colleague said, "Now wait a second; let me try to help you get organized." Using a pad of sticky notes, she helped him to break down the aspects of the project. After only ten minutes, he really felt like he could do the project after all.

This is the beauty of the work breakdown structure, which looks like an organizational chart. It's a way to break the project down to smaller, more manageable pieces starting at the top and working down. We don't manage a project. We manage the small pieces. The work breakdown structure is the foundation of everything we do to organize the project. You will see that team members, managers, sponsors—everyone—gets really excited when they see a work breakdown structure or they help create one.

From a project manager's point of view, you get a chance to double check: Are you on the right track? Do you understand what is expected of you? Does the team understand what it will take to accomplish the work of the project? Keep in mind that a work breakdown structure might be something that takes you a little while to get used to.

Imagine a list such as this for a project to build a house:

- Select the location of the house
- Pour the foundation
- Frame the interior
- Drywall the walls
- Put on roof
- Rough out and install the utilities

> **Work Breakdown Structure (WBS)**
>
> A deliverable-oriented "family tree" of work packages that organizes, defines, and graphically displays the total work to be accomplished to achieve the final project objectives

- Design and install landscaping
- Finish the interior

Many project managers make lists like the previous one for things that need to be done to accomplish the project. If you are one of those people, ask yourself how comfortable you are that your list is complete. Would you stake your reputation or your job on it? The answer is probably no. Therefore, you spend the entire duration of your project not sure if you have everything, not sure if you will meet any required completion date or cost. Not being sure adds unneeded stress and provides no value to the project.

If you have been making lists, give a list to someone who is not involved in your project and is not a technical expert. Ask them if they understand the project from looking at the list. In my own informal research, the answer is always no!

What about a list like this one?

Site
- Survey
- Layout
- Grade

Foundation
- Erect forms
- Pour concrete
- Remove forms

Framing
- Frame roof
- Floor joists
- Sub-floor
- Stud walls

Walls
- Drywall and tape

Roofing

Utilities
- Water
- Gas
- Electric

Landscaping
- Design
- Install

Finishing Work

No, it still does not help people understand the project. Yet, watch out! In other project management books and classes, such a list is often given as an example of what to do. It should be an example of what NOT to do.

Such a list will not be complete and does not help communicate what is the project. There is another choice. What if you could take the project and break it down into smaller, more manageable pieces that you were sure would add up to the entire project? What if you had a way to gain input on this subject from many contributors to really make sure you have all the pieces of scope? Would that be valuable?

The need for a complete understanding of the work to be done on the project goes beyond scope and into time and cost. Coming up with realistic time and cost estimates involves estimating all the work, not just most of it. Even staffing a project requires that all the work be understood in advance, so that the right staff is acquired for the project.

The Work Breakdown Structure

The tool to receiving all these benefits is not a list, but a work breakdown structure, also referred to as a WBS.

The WBS is used to define or decompose the project into smaller, more manageable pieces. It may look like an organizational chart, but that is where the similarity ends. The WBS is created with the team from the top of the chart down to the bottom.

A WBS looks like this:

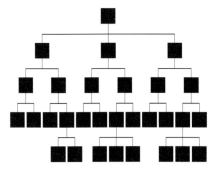

How to Create a WBS To create a WBS, start at the top by breaking your project into pieces. The first row can contain any words that describe the major pieces of the project, and must completely define the project.

A WBS focuses on deliverables (work that needs to be done on the project) but does not need to be organized that way. From working with thousands of people in creating WBSs for the real world, the best way to describe the first level is to break the project down by its life cycle. Here are a couple of examples:

WBS for building a house:

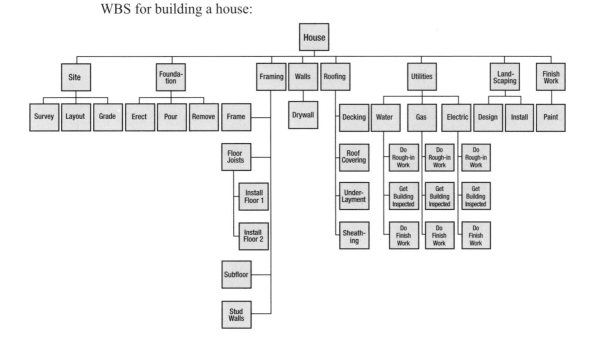

WBS for a software development project:

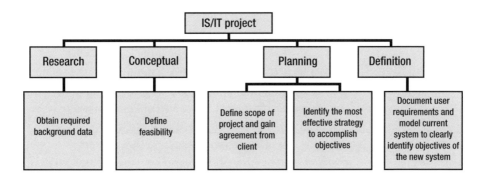

Work Package

The lowest level of a WBS

It contains a collection of work activities that can be assigned to a specific team or individual for execution of the work

Notice that this level of the WBS fits into how the work will be done and should match the life cycle described in the project scope statement. This life cycle approach helps make the WBS understandable to all and provides a foundation for reusing the upper parts of the WBS for other projects. In other words, the life cycle approach will make the upper parts of WBSs for many projects within a department the same.

Once the first level of the WBS is created and deemed complete, each of the boxes is broken down further into two or more pieces, and those are each broken down further into two or more pieces until a small piece of work is reached. The lowest level of a WBS is called a work package.

Here is an example of breaking down the top level of the WBS, starting with the box identified as "Definition" in the previous WBS example.

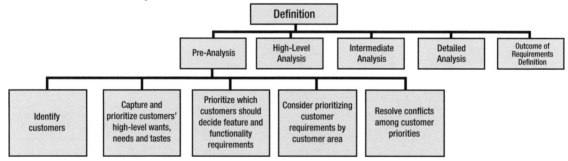

What Size Should a Work Package Be?
The project manager must decide to what level to control the project. On huge projects, it may not make sense for the WBS to be broken down to work packages expected to take 80 hours to complete, as this will create too many things to manage and too much unnecessary reporting. What about 200-hour work packages? The decision is up to the project manager; however, the following is a general rule.

For most projects, small work packages are defined as work that:

- Can be realistically and confidently estimated
- Cannot be logically subdivided further
- Has about 8 to 80 hours worth of effort, or whatever makes sense for your project
- Has a meaningful conclusion and deliverable
- Can be completed without the need for more information
- May be outsourced or contracted

Milestone

A significant event or checkpoint within the project schedule

The size of work packages also relates to reporting periods and project control. One of the mistakes people make in managing projects is to ask, "What percent complete are you?" In most cases, the person being asked this question will think, "Percent complete of what? I am not sure what we are doing! Let me just come up with a number that will make the project manager happy!" Does this happen to you? Well, one of the problems in this situation is a lack of clear definition of the work, which is solved by a WBS and a WBS dictionary (described later in this chapter). Instead of asking, "What percent compete are you?" wouldn't it be great to be able to ask, "Are you done yet?"

Another problem is the work is too large. Having small pieces of work is like having milestones. Both are ways to control the project, because if the milestone is reached or the work is completed on time, then the project might be in good shape.

TRICKS OF THE TRADE To gain the benefits of added control on the project, determine in advance how far off the schedule you can be and still make it up. Then make the work packages on your project no larger than that. In other words, if you have planned in flexibility that you can make up a two-week delay, make the average work package no more than 80 hours. Then you can focus on "Are you done yet?" and produce clear and accurate reports on the status of your project.

Tricks for Creating the WBS

TRICKS OF THE TRADE: The WBS is created with the team, but it may also be done with other stakeholders or the sponsor present. This trick is especially helpful if the sponsor does not understand the work that needs to be done, or thinks it will take only a short amount of time. Having them present (but not contributing) during the WBS creation will help later if the project manager needs to explain that the work required will take longer than the sponsor or stakeholders desire.

Another benefit of having the stakeholders or sponsor present while creating the WBS is to prevent the team from going beyond what the stakeholders or sponsor want. Though it is more common for the sponsor or stakeholders not to understand all the work needed, it is also possible that the project manager could see the work as something more expansive than the stakeholders or sponsor want. The sooner this is discovered, the better.

The first time you create a WBS may be hard, as it is a new way of looking at scope, and a new tool. Give yourself time. Here are some tricks to make it easier:

TRICKS OF THE TRADE: The best method to create a WBS is to use sticky notes with the team to break the project down (decompose the project) into smaller, more manageable pieces.

TRICKS OF THE TRADE: Though human resources may not be completely identified at this stage, it is best to create a WBS with as close as possible to the final team, as a group. At a minimum, this improves buy-in and project quality, and decreases project risk.

TRICKS OF THE TRADE: The project manager should create the top level of the WBS before meeting with the team. It will give the team direction, let them see what a WBS is, and prevent wasted efforts.

TRICKS OF THE TRADE: Add only work that is needed to complete the project deliverables. Do not include extra activities.

TRICKS OF THE TRADE To break each level down further, ask "What do we need to do for this item in the WBS?" Or "What does ____ mean for this project?"

Keep in mind that each level of the WBS is a smaller segment of the level above, and that the entire project is included in each of the highest levels of the WBS. Some levels will eventually be broken down further than others.

All of the work should be included in the WBS. If it is not in the WBS, it is not in the project!

Don't Forget Research and Evaluation

What many people miss is work that may not be required by the sponsor, but is part of the work that really needs to be done. I refer to this work as research and evaluation. Research is usually the first step in the life cycle that many people forget. It includes reviewing available data (the historical information as discussed in Chapter 6 of this book) and reviewing the project-specific data before jumping in to do the work. Performing this activity makes the rest of the project work faster and easier.

Evaluation of how things went and the creation of lessons learned after the project is completed are hugely valuable in improving future projects. Therefore, evaluation must be included somewhere in every WBS.

When a project is done, it may not really be done. There needs to be some technical transition of the project to those who will manage the product of the project. This transition is also often forgotten in project life cycles.

Exercise:

Now it is time to apply what you have learned. Let's create a WBS for the project of moving to another city. You have received a job offer in that city, and want to plan the move.

Answer:

Remember that every WBS can be different depending on the understanding of the scope of the project. In this case, we do not have much of a scope and certainly not a scope statement or project charter. But the WBS might look like this:

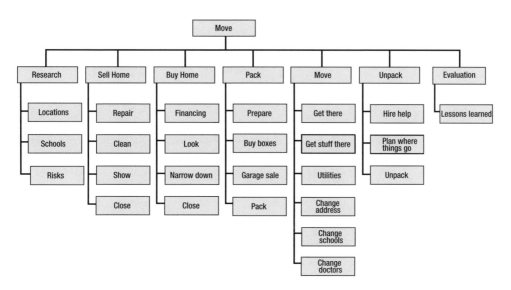

Much of what goes into a WBS will be based on the team's experience. I have had the pleasure of moving repeatedly in my life, and I would certainly argue strongly for the inclusion of "familiarize yourself with the new neighborhood" as a branch in the WBS. You might have included other items. If the WBS were done with the team, you would have a discussion about many potential items to include. I think you would also find the creation of a WBS easier and more fun with the team.

It is also important to realize that project management activities can be included in the WBS. When this is done, it is usually listed as its own branch of the WBS and is usually included on projects where a complete cost and time estimates must be created (project management activities will need to be budgeted and scheduled).

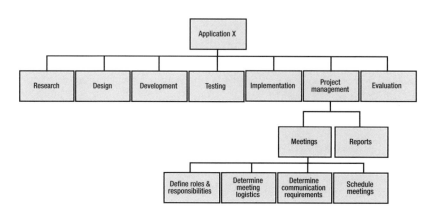

Make sure that each item in the WBS is properly named. Work titled "design completed" can lead to scope creep and misunderstanding because it is too open-ended, whereas work that includes a verb and a noun such as "design the X component" is much more descriptive.

It might be helpful to number each work package to make it easier to track later. When the WBS is completed, code numbers are assigned to help distinguish where a work package is in the WBS. There are many different numbering schemes one can use, but generally they look like this:

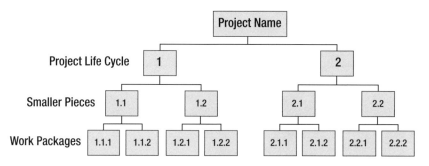

Why Bother Creating the WBS?
Remember that it is better to estimate a project at the smallest (work package) level in order to improve accuracy. This is the benefit of the WBS—that level of detail helps in creating the estimates, as well as staffing the project and

proving how many people are needed. Risks on the project (what can
go right and wrong) are also identified by work package.

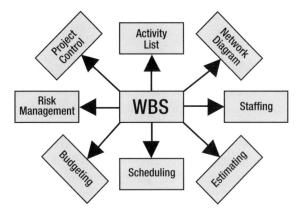

A WBS:

- Forces you to think through all aspects of the project
- Helps prevent work from slipping through the cracks
- Helps people get their minds around the project
- Provides the team members with an understanding of where their
  pieces fit into the overall project management plan and gives them
  an indication of the impact of their work on the project as a whole
- Facilitates communication and cooperation between and among
  the project team and other stakeholders
- Helps prevent changes
- Focuses the team's experience on what needs to be done, resulting
  in higher quality and a project that is easier to manage
- Provides a basis for estimating staff, cost, and time
- Provides PROOF of the need for staff, budget, and time
- Gets team buy-in and builds the team
- Can be reused for other projects

A WBS is so valuable that it should be done even for the smallest
project. All of the following should be done in order to gain full
benefit from the WBS tool.

- Involve the entire team
- Work to pull out the team's ideas during WBS creation
- Include all the work
- Obtain approvals or sign-offs of the WBS
- Publish and distribute the WBS

Common Problems with Creating a WBS

While creating the WBS, many people have difficulty breaking down some parts of the WBS. If this happens to you, realize that it is not a problem with the concept of a WBS, but rather a problem with the clarity of the scope. You must take action to clarify the scope. As you do this, realize that this "problem" is saving you large amounts of time and money that you would have had to spend if this problem was not uncovered until later.

A situation that can arise while creating the WBS is that teams say, "We cannot determine what needs to be done in this branch of the WBS until this other branch is done!" (e.g., they cannot determine how they will develop the software until they complete the requirements analysis). As we discussed in Chapter 5, this is an indication that you have more than one project (e.g., a requirements analysis project AND an implementation project).

Stop right now and reread the last paragraph. Almost every project manager has made this mistake. Just because management identified something as a project does not mean that it is truly just one project. It could be many projects! It is the project manager's responsibility to determine how many projects there are. If you cannot finish a WBS, you probably have more than one project and should break the work down into separate projects. Then, once the requirements are completed, you can start the project(s) to implement them.

Exercise:

What's Wrong with This Picture?

Using what you have learned about creating a work breakdown structure, analyze the example below.

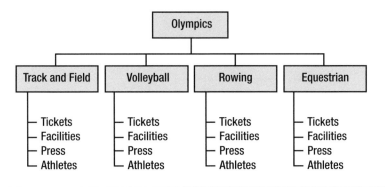

Answer:

This WBS is created by functional areas. When creating a WBS by departments or functional areas, one tends to fit the project into the company, vs. the company into the project. This can result in wasted time, added cost, and a poorly organized project. It also frequently requires many repeats at the third level.

A better idea is to look at the project as an independent effort. If you were to break the project into small pieces, what would they be? Remember, creating a work breakdown structure should help the project be better organized and help you determine all the work that needs to get done, thereby creating a better schedule, budget, and other components of the project management plan. Functional assignments should be done at the work package level, not the top level of a WBS. Also, in the previous diagram, there is no research or evaluation.

Below is a better way to draw a WBS for this project.

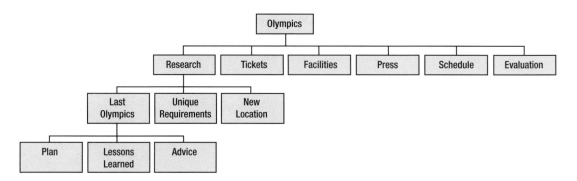

Exercise:

Create a work breakdown structure for your real-world project.

Throughout the Project

Here are more tricks to help you get the most value out of a work breakdown structure.

TRICKS OF THE TRADE If you want to keep a copy of the WBS that was created with sticky notes, take a digital picture and e-mail that to the team and stakeholders.

If you want to record the WBS in the organizational chart format, you can input it into software that creates an organizational chart. Some choices are:

- All Clear (preferred by most)
- Visio (a graphical program)
- WBS Chart (a Microsoft Project add-on)
- MS Office (has an organizational chart feature in the "Insert" tab)

The WBS will continue to provide value throughout the life of the project. The WBS can be used any time the project manager needs to re-evaluate the scope of the project. For example:

- When there is a scope change to the project
- To evaluate any impacts of other changes on scope
- As a way to control scope creep by reminding everyone what work is to be done
- As a communications tool
- To help new team members see their roles

The WBS may be changed and updated throughout the project, and can be used to help stakeholders understand how their pieces fit into the whole project. On very small projects, where a detailed schedule has not been created, work packages in a WBS could be crossed off to show progress.

Contributed by: Rhonda N. Allen
Atlanta, GA

To minimize re-engineering, which often leads to many changes in the project and greatly affects the overall cost of the project, I like to play the "what-if" game during design review. I develop a WBS and a process flowchart for different phases of construction to identify any potential gaps in the plan. I then ask the designer to explain how the design would change if a complication arises in each activity. A clear understanding of the techniques and alternatives available reduces the number of changes in execution. This increases the owner's or sponsor's confidence in the expected product and lays the groundwork for successful negotiations, should change become necessary.

> **WBS Dictionary**
>
> A detailed description of the work to be done for each work package, including scope of the work package, associated activities, milestones and success criteria, as well as any information needed to control the work

The WBS Dictionary

Imagine sending someone an e-mail that says that it is time to start their work package titled "design the interface." Can you imagine the difference in interpretation that can occur between what the project manager wants and what is provided? What about the problems that can occur when the person who is to complete the work package says to himself, "I am not sure what I need to do!"

On large projects, the work packages identified in the WBS may need to be broken down further by those assigned the work packages (e.g., they create their own WBS for the work package, and then break each piece down into its own WBS dictionary.) On smaller projects, each work package needs to be defined in more detail. This is where the WBS dictionary comes in.

The WBS dictionary could possibly be better termed "work package description." Its function is to provide the person completing the work package with a description of the work package, plus any types of control, such as how much the work package will cost to complete, how long the work package may take, and the acceptance criteria for the work package.

Keep in mind that the work package is the level of detail to which the project manager controls the project. The WBS dictionary should contain all the items needed to control the work.

 It is standard practice to have WBS dictionaries. Following is a form, illustrating what a WBS dictionary should include, as well as an explanation of each field.

WBS Dictionary		
Work Package #	Date of Update	Responsible Organization/ Individual
Work Package Description		
Work Package Product		
Acceptance Criteria (How to know if the work is acceptable)		
Deliverables		
Assumptions		
Resources Assigned		
Duration		
Schedule Milestones		
Cost		
Due Date		
Interdependencies	Before this work package	
Interdependencies	After this work package	
Approved by Project Manager		Date

© 2006 Rita Mulcahy • (952)846-4484 • info@rmcproject.com • www.rmcproject.com

Work Package Number On large projects, this number might help keep track of work packages. It has a negative side, though. Giving something a number makes it less personal and therefore easier to forget and not buy into.

Date of Update Work packages, like the rest of the project, could change over time. Document control and configuration management activities require the project manager to make sure everyone has the correct version of any project document. Putting a date on it can help.

Responsible Organization/Individual In order to have accountability, each work package should be assigned to one person to complete. That one person might form a small team to complete the work package, but the project manager would only need to interact with the person assigned the work package.

Work Package Description This section is best created with the help of the person assigned the work package for many reasons:

- The project manager is not required to know how to do all the work on the project, just how to manage the project.
- Quality is much improved when the person who knows how to do the work completes the description.
- Commitment to actually completing the work on time is greatly improved if the person doing the work creates the description of the work. In this case, the work package becomes his or her work package, rather than the project manager's work package.
- The project manager will get a chance to look for scope creep in the description. The description then helps prevent scope creep later, as the work package is being completed.

Work Package Product What is the end result of a work package? Is it a design, or a tested design, or even just the plan for a design? Describing the product of the work package, when the work package description does not do so, helps the project manager be more assured that the complete scope will be done for the work package and also helps decrease the possibility of scope creep.

Assumptions Assumptions made and found later to be incorrect can change the entire design of the project. Therefore, it is wise to document any assumptions made for each work package so that the project manager can review the assumptions to check validity later on in the project.

Resources Assigned On larger projects, the project manager might assign resources to assist the person completing the work package. These resources can be people, equipment, or supplies, and should be described in the WBS dictionary.

Duration When you ask someone to write a WBS dictionary, ask them to estimate duration (and cost) at the same time. The concept of duration will be described in more detail in Chapter 10 of this book.

Schedule Milestones The creation of milestones for the project is another way for the project manager to control the project and to know how the project is doing while the work is underway. If a milestone date is met, the project may be okay. Depending on the project, it might be useful for the person completing a work package to know to which milestone the work package belongs.

Cost See the discussion of duration above.

Risk As you will read in Chapter 13 of this book, risks are the good and bad things that can happen to affect the project. Risks should be identified by work package as well as for the project as a whole. Listing them in the WBS dictionary is a trick for keeping them in focus.

Due Date Once the project management plan is completed, each work package will have a date by which it must be completed without delaying the project. Such a date is listed in the WBS dictionary in order to keep focus on the date and prevent delay.

Interdependencies It is often helpful to know what work comes before and after the work package. Sometimes knowing this will prevent the work package from being delayed because the effect becomes more known—"If I am late, I will delay Jane and her work package that comes next."

Approved by the Project Manager
Approval implies authorization. Without approval, there can be no control.

Throughout the Project

The WBS dictionary is used:

- As a level of control for the project (e.g., Is the work being done on a work package level as described in the WBS dictionary?)
- To determine if a requested change is within the scope of the project
- To prevent scope creep
- To increase understanding of what needs to be done
- To increase buy-in to what needs to be done
- To send to functional managers or resource owners to inform them about what work their people are doing for the project
- As a reporting tool from those assigned the work package to the project manager
- As the high-level basis for the scope of work for any work to be outsourced or contracted

Chances are you had never heard of a WBS dictionary. The chances are also good that in reading the description, you said to yourself, "I do not have time to do all this work." Let's talk about this.

In the real world, scope creep and lack of buy-in are huge problems that can cost the project a huge amount of time, money, and headaches. We have said that project management is about preventing problems rather than dealing with them. The WBS dictionary is a key tool in the fight to manage and control projects. As described above, the WBS dictionary becomes a necessity.

Keep in mind that each WBS dictionary can be created by the person assigned the work package, not the project manager. Therefore, the project manager's work may not take much more time than reviewing each work package, looking for added scope or misunderstanding of scope, and making sure the estimates are reasonable.

It is important to note that the WBS dictionary may be iterated as new information becomes available.

The WBS dictionary is one of those parts of project management that you might have to try before you believe it. When I first heard of the concept, I too was skeptical. Now I would not work on a project without it.

Here are some tricks to make the WBS dictionary work for you.

TRICKS OF THE TRADE. When approved, a final copy of each WBS dictionary is provided to those who will complete the work package work. As the work is being done, team members use the WBS and WBS dictionary to confirm the work they are assigned.

The WBS dictionary can also form the basis for any work package level reporting (e.g., How are you doing in completing the work as described? Does the description need to change? How are you doing in meeting the time or cost estimate? Does the acceptance criteria we created still make sense?).

TRICKS OF THE TRADE. If you still think you will not have enough time, why not use this trick—just create WBS dictionaries for higher levels in the WBS than the work package level. This will create larger pieces, but still provide some level of control and buy-in.

Team Members

Team members can be involved in the work breakdown structure and WBS dictionary. They may:

- Help to break the first level of the WBS down to work packages
- Create, or assist the project manager in creating, WBS dictionaries for work assigned to them

Chapter Summary
Key Concepts
A WBS is:
- A hierarchical way to break a project into smaller, more manageable components or work packages
- A description of WHAT needs to be done
- A way to graphically show what is and what is not in the project in smaller detail
- A major precursor to budgeting, scheduling, communicating, allocating responsibility, and controlling the project

A WBS dictionary:
- May be written by the person assigned to the work package
- Includes a description of the work package product
- Includes information needed to control the work

Questions for Discussion
How does a WBS dictionary help the project manager? How does it help the team?

Why should project management activities be included in the WBS?

Action Plan

What you will do differently in your real-world project management
as a result of reading this chapter?

Let's save you an immense amount of time. Instead of talking about estimating by covering pages of needless information, let's talk about the real world. If we are to put estimating in focus, it involves getting a realistic estimate, not just any estimate.

Many project managers create time or cost estimates without much support for the process, primarily because the estimates they have been able to create in the past have been so unreliable. Let's see if we can help you prevent such a problem. First, take the time to describe the specific difficulties you have seen in the real world with estimates.

Real-World Problems with Estimating on Projects

Depending on your experience, you might have included such things as:

- Estimates include a pad
- All the work is not estimated
- Misunderstanding of the work to be done
- Estimates are created by the wrong people
- Estimates change for no apparent reason
- Actual time or cost is very different than the estimate

When you are finished, go to the free Web site, (www.rmcproject.com/crash), and submit your list. You will then get a chance to see other's lists. Imagine the value of seeing the problems others have faced, so you might avoid the same problems on your own projects! The first important lesson is that estimating is not an isolated activity in project management. What has been done before you ask for estimates will directly affect the quality of the estimates.

Let's try it out. Review the following list of problems with estimates, and think about tools or techniques we have discussed that would prevent those problems. Really apply what you have learned while completing this exercise.

Exercise:

Problem	How to Prevent It
Estimates include a pad.	
All the work is not estimated.	
There is a misunderstanding of the work to be done.	
Estimates are created by the wrong people.	

Estimates change for no apparent reason.	
Actual time or cost is very different than the estimate.	

Answer:

Problem	How to Prevent It
Estimates include a pad.	• Clearly define work packages in the WBS dictionary. • Ask for the team members' opinions, and involve them in estimating from the beginning so there is better trust. • Explain to the team that padded estimates result in a schedule that they cannot rely on.
All the work is not estimated.	• Make sure the WBS is complete. • Make sure there is an estimate for each work package in the WBS.

There is misunderstanding of the work to be done.	• Make sure the team member responsible for the work is involved in creation of the WBS dictionary. • Make sure work packages are defined in the WBS dictionary.
Estimates are created by the wrong people.	• Make sure the team member responsible for the work package is involved in estimating it.
Estimates change for no apparent reason.	• Do not allow estimates to be changed without a reason or without control of the project manager.
Actual time or cost is very different than the estimate.	• Use historical estimates as a sanity check. • Make sure the team member responsible for the work package is involved in creating the WBS dictionary. • Use three-point estimating. • Re-estimate during the project. • Include this topic in a team meeting.

Certainly there could be many "answers" in the right hand column, many of which we will discuss in the following pages. For now, are you starting to see a trend? Did you notice that proper use of the WBS and WBS dictionary can help to avoid many of the problems listed? Many problems with poor estimates are directly related to the lack of a project management process, not an inability to estimate!

Imagine the following version of what can happen in the real world.

A project manager asks a team member to tell her how long some work will take. The team member says to himself, "I do not know exactly what work the project manager is talking about! I have to say

© 2006 Rita Mulcahy • (952)846-4484 • info@rmcproject.com • www.rmcproject.com

something, so I'll take a guess and then double it."

The project manager takes this and other similarly derived estimates and creates a schedule. Later she wonders why the schedule is unrealistic.

Let's talk about estimating in the real world, the way it should be done.

A project manager has built up a level of trust with the stakeholders (including the team members). That trust is based on the project manager caring about the needs of the stakeholders and what they want to get out of the project (or, in the case of team members, what they want to gain by working on the project). The project manager has shown integrity in trying to achieve these things for the team members and other stakeholders.

During the project management process, the project manager has asked the team members, rather than telling them, what must be done to complete the project. The team has therefore had the opportunity to be involved in and buy into the project.

Instead of hearing someone say, "I do not know what you want me to do!" the project manager has created, or has had team members create, a WBS dictionary. Therefore, the work needed for even small pieces of the project has already been described. Under these circumstances, how would a project manager ever encounter a team member saying, "I do not even know what work the project manager is talking about! I have to say something, so I'll take a guess and then double it."

When proper project management is followed, more realistic estimates can be created. Team members are no longer forced to pad their estimates to accommodate unknowns, because the WBS dictionary has accurately described the work that needs to be done. Therefore, it is correct to say that padded estimates from team members are a sign of incompetent project management!

If you have had padding problems in the past, go back and reread the previous paragraphs to make sure you understand what was said and how to prevent the need for padding. In the real world, the project manager needs to put all the estimates and all the pieces of a project together into a cohesive whole that meets the customer's needs. There is no room for hidden pads in real-world project management.

So, how do we estimate in the real world? The project manager lays the groundwork for getting good estimates by first identifying the stakeholders, and when coming up with a project scope statement. One thing leads into another. This preliminary work is critical to the accuracy of the estimates. If the right stakeholders have been identified, and have had input into the requirements and the project scope statement, the resulting estimates based on that project scope statement will be more accurate.

Imagine you have the stakeholders, requirements, project scope statement, WBS, and WBS dictionaries before you start estimating. Is that enough? No! Now you need to follow good estimating techniques.

Work must be properly estimated. Let me cut to the point and tell you the secrets to gaining a good estimate.

- Have the estimates created by those who will do the work
- Estimate small pieces so that the overall project estimate will be more accurate
- Prevent the desire to pad the estimate, by providing or encouraging the creation of a firm description of the work to be estimated
- Have a connection between the work estimated and the cost, so as to better determine changes later
- Document the estimate, and keep it in focus to prevent scope creep
- Make sure you understand effort (how long the work will take without interruption) and duration (over how long a time span the work will be completed), as well as how much it will cost to complete the work

- Record any assumptions
- Record variables, and turn them into identified risks
- Let those doing the estimating know how refined their estimates must be (e.g., high-level or final)

Three-Point Estimate

An estimate calculated based on the optimistic, pessimistic, and most likely estimates for an activity or for a project

Three-Point Estimating

Now imagine the real world. You and the team members have done everything you can to describe the work. Does that mean you and the team can determine an exact time or cost? Maybe, but maybe not. There can still be variables. The point is to not force the team members into hiding those variables from the project manager. Instead of asking for a single estimate, the project manager might say to each team member who is providing estimates, "We have done all we can to clarify the work, but even now things can go right and wrong. So, instead of forcing you to pad your estimate and thereby create a project schedule or budget that is of no use, tell me the following:

- "If everything you can think of goes right, how long will this piece of work take? How much will it cost?" (Optimistic estimate)
- "What if everything you can think of goes wrong? How long will it take? How much will it cost?" (Pessimistic estimate)
- "Most likely, how long do you think it will take? How much will it cost?" (Most likely estimate)

The project manager will learn the amount of variability in the estimates, and the team members will not have to hide the truth.

The project manager can use his or her knowledge of project management, as well as technical knowledge, to DO SOMETHING about the causes of the variability in the estimates, rather than just compiling individual padded estimates into a schedule or budget. The project manager and the team can work together, through the risk management process, to eliminate some causes of variability and thereby improve the estimates or decrease the length or cost of the project. They can then build a schedule or budget based on reality, rather than hiding potential problems. Isn't this better than compiling

---

individual padded estimates into a schedule or budget?

What should you do with those three estimates and the variability in the estimates? Specific reasons for the variability in the estimates are identified and eliminated or reduced as part of the risk management process described in Chapter 13 of this book. This can then lead to re-estimating some of the work. Once the final three estimates for each piece of work are completed, you can:

- Use only the pessimistic estimates to create a project estimate
- Show management three project estimates (optimistic, pessimistic, and most likely), so they are familiar with the range of possibilities
- Use software to perform a Monte Carlo analysis. Such analysis simulates the outcome of the project by making use of the three-point estimates to produce the probability of completing a project on any specific day or for any specific cost. (See the following diagram.)

A Monte Carlo simulation might produce a diagram that looks like this:

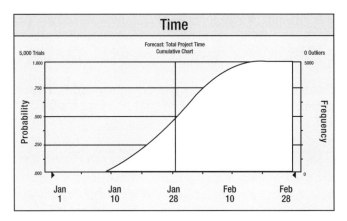

Interestingly, I include a discussion about how to estimate even when I teach very advanced project management classes. The information in this chapter is the real information that produces a realistic estimate; this is the secret to understanding estimating without spending a week in an estimating class, this is what really makes a difference. Unfortunately, most project managers do not know this.

All other topics you can learn about estimating only add marginal additional value.

Throughout the Project

A great project manager will continually look for indications that estimates need to be revised or might be faulty. For example, if the actual time or cost for one work package differs greatly from its estimate, a project manager might investigate all the estimates for similar work, or other estimates from the same estimator. Notice what I said. The project manager should be looking for this. That implies that the project manager should have time for such activities, and that such activities are valuable.

On longer projects, the project manager could re-estimate all future work to double check the accuracy of estimates against current information.

Major deviations in time or cost, or missing a schedule milestone, or major risks occurring that were not identified are all indications that the entire project needs to be re-estimated.

Remember, if the estimates are off for time or cost, this can result in changes to the other parts of the "triple constraint."

Time estimates are used to formulate a schedule (discussed in the next chapter of this book). Cost estimates are used to formulate a budget.

Creating a budget is generally a straight exercise in adding up the cost estimates and adding contingency reserves for risk. Therefore, it is not covered as a separate chapter in this book. Keep in mind that a good budget will break down costs by work package, and will be usable to track total costs throughout the life of the project. Some budgets may include indirect costs such as overhead, but all should include contingency reserves. (Contingency reserves are further discussed in Chapter 13 of this book.)

Team Members

The team members' role in estimating is to:

- Provide honest and truthful estimates
- Work in collaboration with, rather than against, the project manager
- Let the project manager know if any aspect of the estimate changes before it impacts the project

Chapter Summary
Key Concepts
Real-world estimating:
- Is dependent on work done previously in project planning, particularly the WBS and WBS dictionary
- Should be done by those doing the work
- May need to be revised later in the project

Questions for Discussion
How can a project manager prevent padding in project estimates?

What are the benefits of three-point estimating?

How is risk management related to estimating?

Action Plan

What you will do differently in your real-world project management as a result of reading this chapter?

Did you notice that creating a schedule is NOT the first thing to do when you are assigned a project? Often management asks for a schedule because they do not know what else to ask for, and it is the only logical thing they can ask for that will help them believe that work is actually being done on the project.

TRICKS OF THE TRADE If management asks for a schedule at the onset of the project, reply, "If we are going to make this project a success, there are certain things I will need in order to come up with a believable schedule." Then ask for the data needed to create a project charter and scope statement.

Another problem that can occur is that management thinks that project management means just opening some software called "project management software" and following what it says. Most software sold under the title of "project management software" provides only scheduling, reporting, and what-if analysis capabilities; these programs do not document all of the project management that should be done, or all the forms that might be created.

With this in mind, all project managers use some form of software to create a schedule, even if it is done in spreadsheet software using simple symbols to show when work will be done. The purpose of this book is not to explain how to use any software, nor to recommend any particular application. This chapter will give you some tricks for creating a realistic schedule from the data already acquired in the project management process.

On many projects, scheduling is the first time software is used. To create a schedule:

1. Enter the following into "project management software:"
    *   Project start date
    *   Work packages or smaller components, called activities, derived from the WBS
    *   Resource names for each activity (or skills for larger projects)
    *   Estimate for each activity
    *   Predecessor for each activity—what activity or activities must be done before this one can start

Generally, "project management software" takes this data and helps you create two things; a network diagram and a schedule. The network diagram shows which activities are dependent on others and how the project will flow from beginning to end, and is shown below.

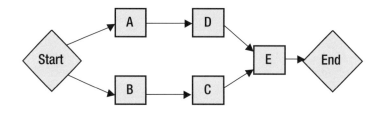

According to the network diagram, the activity represented by C will be completed after activity B. Activity B is therefore said to be a predecessor of activity C. In other words, activity C is dependent on the completion of activity B in order to get started. Can you see how the network diagram helps get the project organized? Everyone can see how the work will flow from beginning to end.

The software can also take the dependency data and start dates and produce an initial schedule, called the schedule model, as shown next. This is the basic schedule you will work from and refine into the final schedule.

Critical Path

The longest path in the network diagram

It helps you prove how long the project will take

ID	❶	Activity Name	Duration	Start	Finish	Predecessors	Resource Names	November				
								Oct 22,'06	Oct 29,'06	Nov 5,'06	Nov 12,'06	Nov 19,'06
1		Start	0 days	Sat 10/28/06	Sat 10/28/06			◆ 10/28				
2		A	5 days	Mon 10/30/06	Fri 11/3/06	1	Dale					
3	▦	B	4 days	Mon 10/30/06	Thu 11/2/06	1	Jeff					
4	▦	C	7 days	Tue 11/7/06	Wed 11/15/06	3	Mary					
5	▦	D	3 days	Fri 11/10/06	Tue 11/14/06	2	Kerry					
6	▦	E	5 days	Thu 11/16/06	Wed 11/22/06	4, 5	Connor					
7		End	0 days	Wed 11/22/06	Wed 11/22/06	6						◆11/22

2. Compare the end date that the software shows to any end date requested by the customer.
3. If the date falls within the range requested by management, add milestones to the schedule as a way for the project manager to control and confirm progress on the project.
4. If it does not fall within that range, look for options to change the schedule by working with the project's critical path (the longest path through the schedule that accomplishes the project in the shortest time). Some options are to:
    -   Decrease risks on the project (see Chapter 13 of this book)
    -   Remove scope
    -   Change the scope so that it takes less time
    -   Have more work done in parallel so the project gets completed faster
    -   Add resources to the project
5. Present those options to management and gain approval, or inform management that the date cannot be reached and provide a proposed alternative date.

The project manager is ethically bound to not blindly accept the end date requested. BEFORE the project work starts, he or she confirms that the requested date can be met. In addition, the project manager meets with management to let them know what it will take to meet any end dates desired. These are not optional activities, but basic project management.

Notice as you are reading this book how many of your preconceived notions about project management are being questioned. Now is the time to improve your knowledge so that you no longer fall into the common traps others face.

When a project is authorized, there is usually an informal or formal decision made by management regarding how much the project is worth to the company (measured in resources, cost, or time). When project management is not used to properly plan a project, there is a huge danger that the project will use more company resources than it is worth. This is one of the reasons projects are cancelled before they are completed.

The length of time the project will take must be determined before work on completing deliverables begins. Any difference between estimated and desired dates must be reconciled. Therefore, the project manager must be able to come to management and not just report that the requested date can or cannot be met, but also provide options about what it will take to make it happen. Stop here for a second, and think about what has just been said. A main job of a project manager is to "make it happen." The science of project management provides the project manager with the tools to determine options. This should be an expected function of project management, but unfortunately it is done so rarely in the real world by new project managers that such abilities are unexpected by management.

To put this in action, a project manager might say, "You want the project completed within six months. We have taken into account the stakeholders' requirements, and the minimum amount of time it will take to complete the project is nine months. However, using project management techniques, we have analyzed the project and discovered that if we delete requirement B from the IT department and requirement X from the Engineering department and add one more programmer to the team, we will then be able to make the six month date. Can you work with me to get these changes approved, or would you like to plan the project to take nine months?"

This phrasing provides management with information they need to make informed decisions, rather than just being told it can or cannot be done. Even more importantly, it prevents a project from being started that cannot meet its end date. This is an example of where management can be involved and support the project in a beneficial manner. Note how productive such actions are, as opposed to making the six-month schedule happen, and letting the IT and Engineering departments find out at the last minute that their requirements are not included in the project.

The essence of scheduling is not the use of software, but the application of what-if analysis—the determination of what we can do to meet the desired end date. It is not about waiting to see what happens. Scheduling is proactive. With so many options to decrease the schedule, having an unrealistic schedule just shows a lack of project management. An unrealistic schedule is the project manager's fault if he or she is not following this process.

TRICKS OF THE TRADE® Giving team members a chance to approve the final schedule helps increase buy-in to the schedule and uncover any items the project manager might have missed.

Exercise:

Let's put this all together by completing the following exercise.

Exercise Data: Your project planning so far has resulted in estimates and a network diagram as shown below:

Activity	Predecessor	Duration in Weeks
Start	None	0
A	Start	4
B	A	2
C	B	10
D	A	15
E	C	16
F	C	16
G	C	15
H	F	6
I	G	9
J	H, I	1
K	D, J, E	6

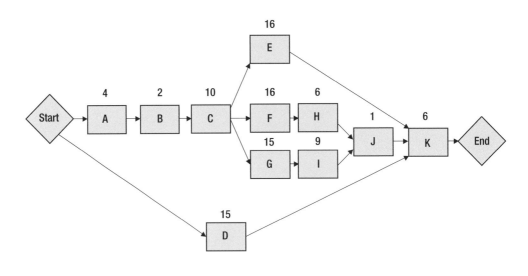

There are four paths through this network:

- Start, A, D, K, END totaling 25 weeks
- Start, A, B, C, E, K, END totaling 38 weeks
- Start, A, B, C, F, H, J, K, END totaling 45 weeks
- Start, A, B, C, G, I, J, K, END totaling 47 weeks

The Question: Based on the information above, the longest or critical path is Start, A, B, C, G, I, J, K, END. This path has a duration of 47 weeks. However, management has stated that the project must be completed in 43 weeks. Based on the options below, which would you select to meet management's requirements and save 4 weeks?

Option	Effect on Time	Effect on Cost	Effect on Scope	Effect on Quality	Customer Satisfaction	Effect on Risk
Option 1	Part of the scope for D could be cut, resulting in D taking 12 instead of 15.	$20,000 savings	Decrease	None	Huge decrease	Slight decrease
Option 2	E could be done after B rather than C.	None	None	None	None	Huge increase

| Option 3 | The work in G could be outsourced to a company more experienced with the work, resulting in G taking 11 rather than 15. | $30,000 savings | None | Increase | None | Slight Increase |
| Option 4 | H could be done by another person in your company who has more experience. This would change its duration from 6 to 4. | $28,000 increase | None | Slight increase possible | None | None |

| Option 5 | The work in F could be completed a different way than currently planned, using older technology but still meeting requirements. F would then take 14 rather than 16. | $4,000 savings | Change | None | None | Decrease |

Answer:

Did you just pick option 3? Then you missed something. Read on!

Options 1 and 2 are not good choices because they are not on the critical path. These options would have no impact on the duration of the critical path, and so would not give you the time savings needed.

Option 3 seems to be the best option until you realize that it really only saves 2 weeks. Although the duration of activity G changes from 15 to 11 weeks, resulting in a decrease of 4 weeks, such a decrease on this path makes another path the longest one. The change to activity G makes path Start, A, B, C, F, H, J, K, End, with a duration of 45 weeks, the longest or critical path. So, this option changes the project length from 47 to 45 weeks. This is a good first step, but it does not save us enough time. We need to keep looking.

At first glance, options 4 and 5 do not deal with the critical path and so do not look like good choices. However, remember that because we have selected option 3, we are now dealing with a new critical path (Start, A, B, C, F, H, J, K, End). Selecting option 3 made the critical path duration 45 weeks. We need to get it to 43 weeks by saving at least two more weeks. Options 4 and 5 now affect the critical path. Let's see if either is a good choice in combination with option 3.

Option 4 saves 2 weeks on the new critical path, but it has a $28,000 cost increase. Why increase cost if we do not have to? Option 5 saves 2 weeks on the new critical path and also saves $4,000 and results in decreased risk.

As a result, the best choice is a combination of options 3 and 5.

IN
THE
FIELD | *Contributed by: Kathy Phillips*
Winchester, MA

I use this trick on projects where the target date has been mandated (either by law or by management fiat) and the team has to "back into" the project plan. It has proven very useful in both getting business buy-in and educating partners on project management levers.

My trick is to illustrate the constraints imposed using the actual project timeline as opposed to an ideal project timeline (were the date not imposed). I begin by stating that the scope, timeline and resources have been established, and that the only lever the team has in meeting the date is quality. I then overlay the actual and ideal timelines on a chart and show two points on the timescale: where we would anticipate all defects to be identified, and where we would expect to have them all fixed. For example, the project might have an ideal timeline where testing runs four months—say, from January to April—but the actual timeline is only two months. Ideally, we would have completed testing and identified defects by mid-March and fixed defects by mid-April. In the real world, we won't have even identified them all, never mind fixed them.

We work closely with business partners to prioritize defects and build workarounds for each. The business then determines if they are willing to "go live" given the total number of workarounds they will need to implement. This creates a partnership and makes joint ownership of the result clear. It also assures that the business is truly prepared, that expectations are managed, and that a post-implementation work queue is identified and prioritized.

Throughout the Project

Smart project managers will realize that a schedule is only an estimate. As we discussed in Chapter 10 of this book, the schedule may need to be recompiled during the project to make sure end dates can be met. Then, when the schedule is approved, the project manager must ensure the project is kept on track to meet the schedule date and associated milestones.

Following are some tricks to help you with schedule management.

TRICKS OF THE TRADE. Remember that your project management activities should include more than just managing the schedule. People new to project management often make the mistake of spending all their time managing the schedule, when the other activities in this book dealing with prevention of problems would have a greater impact. That said, you still need to manage the schedule.

TRICKS OF THE TRADE. Make sure everyone knows what the current schedule is. Highlight the person's name, or put a handwritten message on the schedule, so the schedule is noticed when it is received by each team member.

TRICKS OF THE TRADE. Look for significant changes in work package due dates that result from schedule updates, and make sure those doing the work packages are aware of the new dates.

Send copies of the schedule to team members' bosses, to make sure the resources will be available and to prevent resources from being lost.

 Look for the need to move resources around as a result of changes in the schedule.

 Contributed by: Mary M. Bagley
Williamsville, NY

By the end of business on Thursdays, I send out an e-mail to all key team members and sponsors giving an update on the project. The format is as follows:

> *Hello Everybody:*
> *We are about X percent complete on our project and have X weeks until go-live. We are where we planned to be/behind/or ahead of schedule at this time. Thanks to everyone for our success so far!*
>
> *Attached are the status report, calendar, and high-level project schedule for the XXXX Project.*
>
> *I also attached a vacation calendar for your review. Please let me know of your vacation plans.*

I then list the open action items, issues documented that week, as well as decisions made that week, who made them and when.

This trick sends the same message to all parties involved and gives folks time to respond before the weekend. I can then use the weekend to update the project schedule. The responses received give me time to react to surprises, too.

Team Members

Project managers create the schedule. Team members' involvement may include:

- Confirm that the calendar dates that result from their estimates are acceptable
- Help to determine options for shortening the schedule
- Support the project manager's efforts to meet with management and avoid an unrealistic schedule

Chapter Summary

Key Concepts

A realistic project schedule:
- Is dependent on the accuracy of work done earlier in the project (project scope statement, WBS, estimates)
- Must be determined before project work starts
- May be created with the help of "project management software"
- Directly relates to the other components of the "triple constraint"
- May need to be changed during the project

Questions for Discussion

How does knowing the critical path help the project manager?

What are some of the project manager's options when faced with a required end date that cannot be met?

Action Plan

What will you do differently in your real-world project management as a result of reading this chapter?

| |
| |
| |
| |
| |
| |
| |
| |
| |
| |
| |
| |
| |
| |
| |
| |
| |
| |
| |
| |
| |
| |
| |
| |
| |
| |
| |
| |

I think I thought I heard what I think you said!

Communication is always difficult, especially when you deal with team members you have not met, and/or when team members are from different cultures. When you add bad communication habits to the mix, communication problems on projects get worse.

How many times have you listened to a voicemail message and deleted it before the message was over? How many times have you looked at the beginning of an e-mail, thought it was not relevant, and read no more, only to find out later that there was important information at the end? Such actions only add to communication problems. The key is for you to realize that these are not small problems.

In almost every study, including my own, communication is the number one problem a project manager has on a project. A project manager spends 90 percent of his or her time communicating. Shouldn't we then do something to plan, structure, and control communications?

Recently I was walking in New York City when my husband called me on my cell phone. During our conversation, he said, "It is noisy, where are you?" When I said I was in New York City, he said, "I didn't know you were in New York City. I thought you were at home!" I discovered that we had a communication problem.

The secret to good communication is to realize that communications must be planned in, not random!

The first steps toward good communication have already been taken. Early in the project management process, all the stakeholders have been identified, stakeholder requirements and expectations have been determined, and the scope has been finalized as much as possible.

These basic project management actions have eliminated many communication problems, because scope and requirements are better defined.

Formal communications planning occurs next. This includes determining what needs to be communicated on the project, to whom, when, by what method, and how frequently. It should include analysis of the stakeholders' communications requirements; what do stakeholders want communicated to them, when, by what method, how frequently? (Do you remember the discussion of this topic in Chapter 6 of this book?)

Many project managers think their only role in communication is to issue status reports. Let's go beyond status reports.

Exercise:

What do you think needs to be communicated on a project?

Answer:

A basic list might include:

- Project status
- Project charter
- Project management plan
- WBS
- When resources will be needed
- Meeting schedule
- Work assignments
- New risks uncovered
- Problems
- Changes
- Updates to components of the project management plan
- Upcoming work
- Delays
- Performance

TRICKS OF THE TRADE® More advanced project managers will be concerned with communicating the following:

- Success
- Achievement
- Confidence
- What is worrying team members
- Parts of the project management plan about which team members are unsure
- The date of the next milestone completion party
- Changes to project scope and product scope
- Impacts between the project and other projects

To be effective, communications must include communicating in all the following directions and to the following types of people:

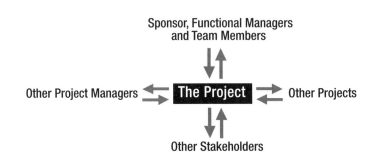

Communication is a two-way street. The project manager must continue to obtain information even as he or she sends it. Let us be very advanced for a minute. Communication is more than sending or acquiring information. It is also about communicating things like the project manager's confidence in his or her own abilities.

So now go back to your list of what needs to be communicated. Can you think of more advanced things that might need to be communicated?

TRICKS OF THE TRADE® What needs to be communicated from the project manager to others?

- Discoveries and lessons learned
- Updates on resources needed, and when
- Changes to the project, and their consequences
- Issue log items from meetings
- That the project manager cares about the project
- The project manager's integrity
- That the project manager is in control of the project
- That the project manager is open to hearing conflicting ideas, problems, and new ideas from stakeholders
- Status of specific requirements
- Schedule for interactions with other departments
- The best way to get information to the project manager
- The best way to find out information about the project

© 2006 Rita Mulcahy • (952)846-4484 • info@rmcproject.com • www.rmcproject.com

What needs to be communicated from others to the project manager?

- Level of commitment
- Happiness
- Changes
- Problems
- Risks
- Areas of confusion
- Hidden agendas
- Bad news
- What they like and do not like about the project
- Areas where they could provide extra help to the project
- Frustrations
- Little things that could become bigger
- Things the project manager missed
- The project manager's performance
- How the project can be improved
- New ideas
- Discoveries
- Lessons learned
- Achievement of milestones

It is time to put it all together into a formal communications management plan. The project manager creates a communications management plan with input from the team. Such a plan might look like this:

What Needs to be Communicated	Why	Between Whom	Best Method for Communicating	Responsibility	When and How Often

Now let's talk about how to communicate. Communications may be formal, informal, written, or verbal, and may be accomplished using any of the following methods:

- E-mail
- Handwritten letter
- Meeting
- Phone call
- Personal conversation
- Overnight delivery
- Report

Communications planning involves asking questions such as:

- Would it be better to communicate the information in an e-mail or telephone call?
- Is this an issue that I should go to see the person about?
- Should I send a letter through the mail in order for it to get real attention?

The process of communications planning forces us to think about the best way to communicate so that we do not send urgent communications by e-mail to someone who never looks at their e-mail; so we do not pick up the phone when we really need to meet with the person we need to communicate with. A major cause of communication problems is simply selecting the wrong method of communication.

Make sure the following items are addressed in your communications management plan:

- Responsibility charts—Who does what? Who should talk to whom?
- How will you interface with other organizations involved in the project?
- How will you interface with the stakeholders?
- What reporting form does the sponsor require?
- What reporting form do you want from the project team?
- How will you clearly delineate project roles and responsibilities?
- What methods should the team use to bring problems or issues to your attention?

Find a partner, and complete the interesting exercise below:

Exercise:

1.	Each of you complete the blank communications management plan for your own real-world project. (10 minutes)
2.	Explain your project in only one paragraph to your partner, and ask what he or she would communicate on your project. DO NOT show your partner your list. (15 minutes)
3.	Repeat step 2, but this time talk about your partner's project and provide your partner with your ideas about what should be in his or her plan. (15 minutes)
4.	Laugh about the good ideas you get, and discuss the aspects of creating a communications management plan that were hard for each of you. (15 minutes)

Take a minute to complete another exercise. Make a list of communication problems you have faced on your projects, and then determine what you can do to prevent similar problems in the future.

Exercise:

Communication Problem	How to Prevent It

Exercise:

How about the following problems?

Communication Problem	How to Prevent It
A team member did not know when his work needed to be done.	
An e-mail was not read in time to take appropriate action.	

The project manager cannot get management to help resolve a technical dispute.	
A team member says she told the project manager about a change to the WBS dictionary, but the project manager has no record of any such conversation.	

Answer:

Communication Problem	How to Prevent It
A team member did not know when his work needed to be done.	Review the communications management plan to see if the team member received an updated copy of the schedule and if he understood how to interpret the schedule.
An e-mail was not read in time to take appropriate action.	Investigate how many e-mails the person receives and review the plan for handling e-mail on your project. Bring such issues up at the next team meeting.
The project manager cannot get management to help resolve a technical dispute.	Let management know how much time and cost the project will incur if the problem is not resolved.

A team member says she told the project manager about a change to the WBS dictionary, but the project manager has no record of any such conversation.	Ask the team member to show that the message was sent. Explain the impact to the project that the problem caused. Ask her for ideas of how to prevent it in the future.

One of the biggest values to you in this chapter may be the ideas on our Web site. Add your problems and solutions to the list at www.rmcproject.com/crash, and gain access to the responses of other project managers from around the world!

IN THE FIELD *Contributed by: Kerry R. Wills*
Hartford, CT

Within project planning, I like to create a "community plan" where a one-page plan is created and then posted on everyone's desktop or a wall. This is a technique that can be used at most points in a project, but upfront is probably the most genuinely received and beneficial.

By contributing to the community plan, team members have ownership of the dates, rather than feeling as though the dates were given to them. People have a hard time committing to activities that they didn't help to plan.

Also, by seeing all of the activities and dates, the team can understand the context of their work and be reminded of when deliverables are due. This seems simple, but oftentimes the plan is hidden away and the team members don't even see it to know what the dates are, or the other activities happening within the project.

Like the town clock of ancient times, all of your "villagers" will be looking at the same clock, and all will know exactly what time it is.

IN THE FIELD *Contributed by: Tim Menke, PMP, Lean Sigma Black Belt*
Rochester Hills, MI

I'm accustomed to managing technical projects staffed with engineers and software developers. I once had the opportunity to take over a struggling Human Resources project in support of a company merger.

The team of HR professionals reacted to my proposed recovery plan, a Microsoft Project Gantt chart, less than enthusiastically. I quickly realized that these folks didn't live in the world of predecessors, successors, float, slack, or even duration, that was commonplace with my technical teams. My disappointment was obvious, but short-lived, as I noticed all of the team members had calendars and/or "to-do" lists in front of them.

I had my project scheduler rerun the same schedule using the calendar month view. I was amazed at how much differently the team reacted to the exact same information in a format that was more familiar and less intimidating to them. I subsequently had 30-60-90 day "look ahead" activity lists printed for each team member, so they could insert them in their planners.

Simply changing the format of the reports enabled me to get the team engaged in planning and executing the project, and provided me with the information I needed to maintain project control. The team members rarely saw the underlying Gantt chart from which their calendars and activity lists were generated, but it was there!

Throughout the Project

Communications planning does not end after the project is planned. It is important for the project manager to revisit the communications management plan and even to solicit comments and changes to the plan throughout the life of the project. Communications require structure and careful thought! If communication is indeed the number one problem on projects, then thinking about managing good communication should be a primary focus of a project manager while the work is underway. Such activities might include using the following tricks:

 Include stories about poor communication, and discussion of communication as an agenda item at team meetings.

 Take the time to ask key stakeholders to identify any aspects of the project they are unsure of, thereby preventing communication problems rather than just dealing with them.

 Update the communications management plan whenever problems or new communication-related needs are uncovered.

 To keep focus on communication problems, add "recent communication problems" to the agenda for team meetings and have those who had the problems describe them.

 Don't forget nonverbal communication. The most sophisticated project managers know that about 55 percent of all communication is not what is said, but how it is said.

Think outside the box! Here are some creative examples of ensuring good communication on projects.

A project manager needed to make sure that someone received and read a report, but the person who was to receive the report was known for not reading them. What did the project manager do? He arranged for a man in a gorilla suit to deliver the report. Naturally, it got noticed!

A project manager had little experience in managing projects and was worried that there was something important that he did not learn while planning the project. Instead of worrying, he decided to hold a contest with a prize for the team member who informed the project manager about the biggest thing he did not know. (See, isn't project management fun?)

TRICKS OF THE TRADE: A project team was loaded down with too many e-mails. Many problems were occurring because people did not get to their e-mail in time, even though they had agreed that this was the best method of communicating the issues. The project manager instituted a new rule that each e-mail should have a 1, 2, or 3 in the subject matter line; 1 for "read it right now," 2 for "read it within two days," and 3 for "I am not sure this affects you, but you should take a quick look at it."

TRICKS OF THE TRADE: A project manager was managing a project that had few objective measures of success. She was concerned about how to determine how things were going. Instead of just holding regular team meetings, the project manager added a new feature. Every other time the team met, the project manager would ask them to rate on a 1 to 10 scale (10 being the highest) how confident they were that the project would be completed on time. She tracked the results and knew when to investigate further and when it was not necessary.

TRICKS OF THE TRADE: Take the trick above, but give the team a way to answer anonymously, or change the question to something like, "How happy are you with this project?" or "What is the probability that there will be a major change on this project?" or "How much fun are you having on this project?" All are relevant questions to uncover areas the project manager needs to investigate. Can you come up with some of your own?

TRICKS OF THE TRADE: A project manager, new to the company, was leading a project. In order to encourage team members to bring issues to him, he handed out pieces of paper to the team at a team meeting. He asked each person to name a hidden objective of the team member sitting to that person's right hand side.

TRICKS OF THE TRADE: In order to communicate success, a project manager set up a "Success" board near her office. Anyone who achieved any of the objectives on the project had his or her picture posted. Naturally, the board was full, and everyone walking by got the impression the project and the team were highly successful.

Winning Trick

Contributed by: Alan E. Feinberg
Rockville, MD

I managed a large multi-disciplined team that was dispersed among various locations. Keeping everyone informed about the program was a prime problem. I found that official e-mails, correspondence, status reports, program reviews, etc. were often ignored by various members of the team, or not fully distributed to all concerned. After I started an informal newsletter, which I e-mailed to all members of the project team, our internal communications greatly improved. Basically, my goal was to convey information without being too heavy about it. I tried to write this newsletter in the style of a "hometown rag," making references to classic rock songs, using colloquial language, and keeping it folksy, humorous and down to earth. In addition to program highlights, status, and other essential management information, I kept the publication human by congratulating people on work and personal achievements, sending holiday and birthday greetings and occasionally including recipes or silly stories. I included trivia on various arcane subjects, and even held contests. In fact, the first contest was to name the newsletter. I also solicited input from the readers and on both professional and non-professional topics and included their contributions in later issues. After awhile, the publication became self-sustaining and virtually wrote itself. My ultimate validation was when I actually got requests from personnel working other programs to be included on our distribution list because it was so informative. Long story short, my newsletter became a must-read publication and was a valuable tool in promulgating information to my team and others in the organization.

Contributed by: C. Poovannan
Hyderabad, Andhra Pradesh, India

When I e-mailed weekly progress reports as attachments to the stakeholders, most of them didn't open the attachments immediately. The result was that crucial information about the project didn't always reach them in a timely manner. In addition, the attachment of lengthy reports added an undue load to the exchange server.

I found the trick of converting the report to an HTML document and sending it directly in an e-mail to the stakeholders. This allowed them to easily access the information in the message itself, rather than in an attachment. Further, I added a column in the progress report which recognized the official/personal achievements of the stakeholders during that week. This was motivating for them, and everybody was happy to see their names reflected in the report, which was read by a large group of stakeholders.

We have experienced massive improvement in project communication using this approach, and this practice is now followed by most of my project management office colleagues in our company. Even the IS team is appreciative that the load on the exchange server has been drastically reduced.

Team Members

Team members' role in communications management can include:

- Let the project manager know what method or form of communication is best for them on the project
- Help to create the communications management plan for the project
- Follow the communications management plan
- Let the project manager know of communication issues that are not addressed in the communications management plan
- Let the project manager know of instances where the communications management plan was not helpful, or was in error
- Work to make sure all their communications are clear and effective
- Keep communication issues at the forefront of their thoughts

Chapter Summary
Key Concepts
Communications:
- Must be planned into the project
- Must meet the needs of stakeholders

Questions for Discussion

Why is it important to have a formal communications management plan?

What things are likely to be forgotten in communications planning?

How should a project manager manage communications throughout the life of the project?

Action Plan

What you will do differently in your real-world project management
as a result of reading this chapter?

Notice what chapter number we are up to? Lucky chapter 13! Is that just a coincidence?

A project manager was excited to be working on one of the most important projects in the company. Partway through the project, a supplier to the project suffered a shutdown of one of their main facilities, thereby delaying shipment to many of their clients. The project manager was leaving work that day when one of his company's senior managers stopped him and said, "How can you be leaving work on time when we have such a major problem to deal with? Shouldn't you be holding some kind of troubleshooting meeting?" The project manager said. "No need; we already have a plan in place for just such an occurrence. No meeting is required. The shutdown will only affect our project slightly!"

How good would you feel if you were this project manager? How exciting would project management be if every day was filled with situations like the one just described? Well, this is what risk management is all about. It is the reason great project managers focus on risk management. A little effort can make a huge difference. It provides an opportunity for the best project managers to really show their stuff, and puts the project manager's and the stakeholders' experience to good use. Read on!

The purpose of risk management is to identify as many potential opportunities as possible, and to plan the project in such a way as to take advantage of these opportunities. However, the short answer in the real world is to find problems before they "hurt" us on the project. Risk management seeks to identify and eliminate as many potential threats to the project as possible, and then to reduce the negative impact of the remaining threats on the project.

Risks

Events that can affect the project for better or worse

Opportunities or threats

When project managers use risk management, they have a plan for what to do if a negative risk that remains on the project occurs (a contingency plan) and even a fallback plan for what to do if the contingency plan does not work.

We perform risk management to be more in control of a project, but there are other benefits. Have you ever thought that risk management might result in a direct and provable decrease in project time and cost? Risk management saves project time and money! To get such results, it is important to realize that there is a process to risk management.

Risk Management Planning Determining how risk management will be done on the project, who will be involved, and procedures to be used

Risk Identification Determining specific risks by project and by work package or activity

Qualitative Risk Analysis Subjectively analyzing the probability and impact of each risk, using a scale of 1 to 10 for each risk. This allows the project manager and the team to narrow down the long list of risks into a short list

Quantitative Risk Analysis Numerically estimating the cost and time impact of the risks

Risk Response Planning Determining what can be done to reduce the overall risk of the project by decreasing the probability or impact of threats, and increasing the probability or impact of opportunities

Risk Monitoring And Control Executing the risk response plan to manage risks and control the overall project risk

As a result of this process, every risk is assigned to someone to manage; that person becomes the risk response owner. Then, when a risk occurs, the risk response owner can take action, with no meeting required! How much time and work would this save on your real-world projects?

When risk management is done on a project, the project manager spends more time implementing contingency plans and fallback plans than holding meetings to determine what to do! The project manager can be proactive rather than reactive, and can spend the entire project feeling that he or she is in control, vs. the project controlling the project manager. Ask yourself if that would be good for you. Can see why so many people are learning risk management techniques?

TRICKS OF THE TRADE: How do you know when you have identified enough risks? Do it until it becomes silly. This might seem like an ineffective trick until you try it. To be really effective, risk identification should involve the identification of possibly hundreds of risks, not just five or ten.

TRICKS OF THE TRADE: Lists of risks should be available from other projects (as part of historical information). When you think you are finished identifying risks on a project, look at historical information in your company about risks past projects have faced. These lists will give you ideas about more risks for your project. Consider examples of things that can go right to help make sure opportunities are identified as well as threats.

IN THE FIELD *Contributed by: Ed Delker, PMP*
Wentzville, MO

Sometimes major stakeholders are less than forthcoming in discussing key business drivers and risks. After setting the stage with a series of open-ended questions about the project from the stakeholder's perspective, if I am getting minimal elaboration from the stakeholder, I'll ask the person, "What kind of things will get you fired?" Or, I might ask what will get their boss fired. The questions have a certain amount of shock value, but they definitely get a stakeholder focused

Risk Register

A document that
includes data on
identified risks to
the project, and the
results of ongoing
risk planning and risk
responses

It is updated throughout
the project

on the personal consequences of not managing risk. This invariably
leads to identification and prioritization of risks that may not come
out of polite conversation.

TRICKS OF THE TRADE. Collect the risk information in a table called a risk register. This
allows documentation so that alternative choices can be made if
one response plan does not work.

Exercise:

Create a basic risk register for your project using the following table.

Things That Can Go Right (opportuntities)				
Risk	P	I	P x I	Response Plan
Things That Can Go Wrong (threats)				
Risk	P	I	P x I	Response Plan

 Now go to our free Web site, (www.rmcproject.com/crash), to
see examples of risks from around the world.

Identifying risks is not enough. Risk efforts will result in going
back and changing the project management plan. For example, the
risk process might involve the deletion of a piece of scope that was
adding too much risk to the project. Therefore, the WBS and maybe
the project scope statement will have to be updated. Schedule and
cost will also be affected by the risk management process. Risk

management will result in many pieces of work becoming cheaper and faster. A team member who has estimated a piece of the project work will be able to narrow the range of that estimate after the risks or uncertainties are diminished for the work. This is a huge concept for the real world. Risk management saves the project time and money!

Once the individual estimates for work are adjusted after the risk management effort, risks will still remain and must be accounted for in the project management process. The risks that remain are added to the project cost and schedule as reserves.

There can be two kinds of reserves on a project; a contingency reserve and a management reserve. The contingency reserve is calculated based on the specific risks that remain in the project after risk management, and can therefore be supported or proven to management. The management reserve is simply a percentage added on to the project to account for risks not identified. This reserve is usually a percentage of the total cost.

Be careful—risk management involves the identification of specific risks. It is not acceptable to add a management reserve without a contingency reserve.

Contingency reserves are not pads, as they are not hidden, and the need for them can be justified and supported. Contingency reserves are designated for specified risks, not something that just happens.

Reserves are a required part of basic project management, not an advanced technique. Risk becomes advanced with the application of more complex techniques for identifying, assessing, and managing risk.

The following exercise illustrates how to calculate a contingency reserve for a project.

Exercise:

You are planning the installation of hardware and software throughout your company. After your risk management efforts to eliminate and reduce risks, you are left with the following risks that remain on the project. How much reserve would be needed for time on the project?

(Note that in the real world, there are likely to be a much greater number of risks remaining. For the sake of simplicity, we have used only four here.)

> A. A 25 percent probability of a 4-day delay in receiving customer approval
>
> B. A 10 percent probability that the equipment installation will take 40 days less than planned
>
> C. A 50 percent probability that two computers will need to be returned for poor quality, causing a 20 day delay
>
> D. A 30 percent probability that a certain expert will become available to work on the project, resulting in a 9-day savings due to increased productivity

Answer:

Did you notice that some of these things are opportunities (good things)? We need to add time for threats (negative risks), and we need to subtract time for opportunities.

Watchlist

Low-rated (non-critical) risks documented for monitoring and review

> A. This is a risk, so we add 25 percent X 4 days (+ 1 day)
>
> B. This is an opportunity, so we subtract 10 percent X 40 days (- 4 days)
>
> C. This is a risk, so we add 50 percent X 20 days (+ 10 days)
>
> D. This is an opportunity, so we subtract 30 percent X 9 days (- 3 days)
>
> The reserve is therefore +1 – 4 + 10 – 3, or 4 days.

The inclusion of this amount of time in the schedule can be supported by describing the work it is meant to cover, just like normal project work. It can also be supported by pointing out that the method of calculation not only takes into account things that can go wrong, but adjustments are made for the things the project manager will make sure go right.

Risk can affect all parts of the project. That is why it is usually left for last in the planning process. It is not until after the WBS is created and after initial scheduling has been done that many risks can be identified.

Throughout the Project

There are things that should be done related to risk while the project is underway. Consider:

- Including risks in communications and as a topic at team meetings
- Revisiting risks that were identified, but were thought of as having too low a probability or too low an impact to warrant

---

responses. These risks are often included on a watchlist and reviewed by the project manager throughout the project to make sure they have not increased in ranking

- Looking for unexpected effects or consequences of risk events
- Re-evaluating risk identification, qualitative and quantitative risk analysis when the project deviates from the plan

Because risk management was done, the project manager can have substantially more time available while the work is in progress. Problems have already been identified and solutions planned. The following tricks will help you keep in control of the project.

 Use the risk register as a way to document data on risk so that it can be used as historical information on other projects.

 Publish your risks. Sometimes just making the risks known helps prevent them from occurring.

 Management and other stakeholders often don't know how to properly be involved with a project and can therefore negatively impact the project by getting in the way. If this happens to you, you could assign these people some of the work to help look out for and manage risks.

 Keep the focus on risk by asking the following questions during team meetings. "What new risks have been identified this month?" "What parts of the project risk response plan need to be improved or changed?"

Include how risks will be communicated in the communications management plan.

Look for new risks when any changes are made to the project.

While the work is being done, the project manager's focus is on managing risks. When project management processes are followed, the team knows what they need to do, buy-in has been received from the stakeholders, scope creep has been minimized, and the project management plan is as realistic as possible. Please take a minute to imagine what your real world will be like if you do real project management.

The benefits of risk management are: more control of the project, fewer hours spent dealing with problems, more hours spent implementing risk response plans, and overall decreased time and cost for the project. Why in your right mind wouldn't you do risk management on your projects? Think of how much better your day-to-day existence would be. Imagine how much more fun projects would be if you could say every time there was some disaster, "We already have a plan for that."

One of the interesting things about risk management is how simple the process is to understand and to implement. With just this high-level review of risk management, you can start to take action on your projects NOW. The real-world effects include having the time to manage more projects, getting out of work on time, having less stress, and having more time to deal with problems that could not have been predicted.

Team Members

Team members' involvement in risk management can include:

- Identify risks (threats AND opportunities)
- Work with stakeholders to identify their risks
- Determine probabilities and impacts
- Determine how to eliminate major risks
- Determine response plans, contingency plans and fallback plans
- Own or manage some risks
- Implement risk response strategies when an identified risk occurs
- Let the project manager know when a problem occurs or may occur which was not identified as a risk
- Help to manage the reserve

Chapter Summary

Key Concepts

Risk management:
- Is a sequential process that must be followed for all projects
- Includes increasing opportunities as well as decreasing threats
- Saves time and money on projects

Questions for Discussion

How can risk management save time and money on a project?

Who should be involved in risk identification?

What is a reserve?

Action Plan

What you will do differently in your real-world project management as a result of reading this chapter?

Common Errors That Can Ruin Your Career

Although many of these mistakes have already been discussed in this book, so many project managers make silly errors that I thought a list of them would be helpful. The list is not in order of importance.

- Thinking an unrealistic schedule should be blamed on management, rather than on the project manager

- Not holding effective meetings, or bothering to ask those who attend meetings if the meetings were effective

- Not realizing there is a process to project management, and that steps taken early in the project prevent problems later in the project

- Thinking project management is an optional activity

- Thinking project management activities add time and cost, rather than saving time and cost

- Thinking software sold as "project management software" is intended to tell people how to manage projects

- Allowing team members to pad their project estimates

- Managing a program as if it was one project instead of many projects

- Not having or using records of lessons learned from past projects

- Forgetting to include some stakeholders in the project planning and management processes

- Not having a project charter

- Not using the project charter to remind people about what is the project

- Not having all the key requirements before starting work on the project

- Not including the stakeholders in project status communications

- Not keeping the project schedule updated, and not delivering that updated schedule to resource owners

- Not having a WBS for all projects

- Failing to involve the entire team in creating the WBS

- Not identifying risks for the project

- Not realizing that time or cost estimates for the project cannot be completed without including the impacts of risk on the project

- Not planning communication

- Not identifying how each stakeholder wants to be communicated with

1. Support the creation of historical records. Historical records include, at a minimum, the WBS, estimates, risks, and lessons learned from every past project. These records are used to better plan, estimate, and manage future projects.

2. Provide a project charter with clear goals and objectives. Include a description of the project (one paragraph), the project manager's name, clearly defined quantitative goals and objectives (i.e., a 10 percent improvement), and an explanation of why the project is being done. The project charter serves as a "target" for the project. The goals and objectives provide a way to measure success.

3. Protect projects from outside influences, changes, and resource stealing.

4. Allow teams the time to properly plan projects. Teams need time to plan projects in order to achieve substantial decreases in project length and cost. A project schedule cannot be delivered in only a few days.

5. Ensure a finalized scope of work before the project starts. There is little excuse for not having a finalized scope of work. Changes made later can cost 100 times more.

6. Prioritize projects within the company or department. Everyone should know which projects are number one, two, three, etc., in priority at any time within your organization.

7. Require that project management be done. Your support of project management is critical for it to be used in your organization. Focus on the project charter, the WBS, and risk management.

8. Run at less than 100 percent capacity. Overtime is not an option, because any one problem will cause massive problems on all projects.

9. Know that you cannot get something for nothing. Although you may not want to believe it, changes in scope, time, and/or cost will impact project scope, time, and/or cost. Do not allow people to ask for little extras and not expect to "pay" for them.

Team Members

Team members even have a role here. Let me tell you a story. A group of team members was learning project management when they stopped the class and said, "None of our managers know any of this." I asked them what they were going to do about it. After I gave them some time to think, they decided to take a copy of the free tip on the RMC Web site (www.rmcproject.com/crash) from which this chapter is derived, have all the team members sign it, and give it to their manager. Instead of the situation being confrontational, the manager accepted the article. After she finished reading it, she approached the team members to ask, "What is a project charter, and why should I get involved with it?" Information breeds understanding. With information, this manager was able to improve her management activities.

What can your team do about improving things in your company?

Remember, this book does not cover all aspects of project management, just the most important ones. But do not make the mistake of reading this book and then moving on to new topics right away. If you truly want to improve your project management, work on these skills for a year or so. After that time period, come back to this chapter and read it again. It will point you to what to do next.

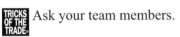 Ask your team members.

Wouldn't it be helpful to have me there with you, after you have learned and used these techniques, to evaluate your performance? Well, I have an even better idea. If you really want to know how you are doing before you move on to continue your learning, ask your team members.

Many people will not feel comfortable talking to you about this in a group setting or in a one-on-one setting. In order to get an honest answer, express your sincere interest in hearing their opinions and then provide many ways they can respond (e.g., by e-mail, a phone call, or in writing). Make sure there is an option for them to reply to you anonymously.

Ask for specific comments regarding the topics in this book. You will be surprised to see just how fast they respond to your request, because chances are they have been thinking about this topic since you started to use professional project management techniques. The topics to include in your survey are, "How have I done in:"

- Understanding the project management process
- Breaking the work into projects
- Gaining, creating, and using historical information
- Identifying and managing stakeholders

- Creating and keeping focus on the project charter
- Creating and managing the project scope statement
- Creating and updating the WBS
- Identifying and managing risk on the project
- Creating and updating the communications management plan
- Avoiding the common errors that can ruin our careers
- Getting our bosses to work on the things they should be doing

Implement the improvements suggested by your team members before moving on to increase your knowledge.

What to Learn Next

So now you are ready to move on. Here are the things you should learn next.

1. Since I focus on what you really need to know to improve your real-world project management rather than just textbook project management, I suggest that you look at my company Web site for online or instructor-led training on more advanced topics. As of writing this book, the best topics to approach are:

   ### Tricks of the Trade® for Project Management
   Fill the gaps in your knowledge of basic and advanced skills in project management
   ### Tricks of the Trade® for Risk Management
   Risk management can make the biggest improvement in your overall project management activities after you learn the basics
   ### What Makes a Project Manager Successful?
   Learn advanced skills of the best project managers from around the world

2. Learning the step-by-step process of project management as described in the table shown earlier and repeated here

Rita's Process Chart

Initiating	Planning	Executing	Monitoring & Controlling	Closing
Select project manager	Determine how you will do planning—part of management plans	Acquire final team	Measure against the performance measurement baselines	Develop closure procedures
Determine company culture and existing systems	Create project scope statement	Execute the PM plan	Measure according to the management plans	Complete contract closure
Collect processes, procedures and historical information	Determine team	Work to produce product scope		Confirm work is done to requirements
	Create WBS and WBS dictionary	Recommend changes and corrective actions	Determine variances and if they warrant corrective action or a change	Gain formal acceptance of the product
	Create activity list	Send and receive information		
Divide large projects into phases	Create network diagram	Implement approved changes, defect repair, preventive and corrective actions	Scope verification	Final performance reporting
Identify stakeholders	Estimate resource requirements		Configuration management	Index and archive records
	Estimate time and cost	Continuous improvement		
Document business need	Determine critical path	Follow processes	Recommend changes, defect repair, preventive and corrective actions	Update lessons learned knowledge base
	Develop schedule	Team building		
Determine project objectives	Develop budget	Give recognition and rewards		
Document assumptions and constraints	Determine quality standards, processes and metrics	Hold progress meetings	Integrated change control	Hand off completed product
	Determine roles and responsibilities	Use work authorization system	Approve changes, defect repair, preventive and corrective actions	Release resources
Develop project charter	Determine communications requirements	Request seller responses	Risk audits	
Develop preliminary project scope statement	Risk identification, qualitative and quantitative risk analysis and response planning	Select sellers	Manage reserves	
			Use issue logs	
	Iterations—go back		Facilitate conflict resolution	
	Determine what to purchase		Measure team member performance	
	Prepare procurement documents		Report on performance	
	Finalize the "how to execute and control" aspects of all management plans		Create forecasts	
			Administer contracts	
	Create process improvement plan			
	Develop final PM plan and performance measurement baselines			
	Gain formal approval for plan			
	Hold kickoff meeting			

3. Working with and managing people on projects

4. Periodically reassessing the project management plan

5. Creating and implementing change control systems

6. Realizing that scope creep is caused by a lack of good project management

7. Determining the need for, and taking corrective actions

8. Dealing with unrealistic schedules and realizing that having an unrealistic schedule is the project manager's fault

9. Meeting management skills

10. Creating and managing baselines for scope, time, and cost

11. Creating and using network diagrams to manage the project

12. Identifying and managing the critical path

13. Creating quality standards to help manage and control the project

14. Measuring progress, including earned value techniques

15. Expanding your change control techniques

16. Learning more about conflict resolution

17. Studying proper project closure

18. Reading about advanced topics such as why projects fail, common errors others make, and expanded discussions on estimating time and cost

19. Identifying and managing float

20. Using Monte Carlo analysis to determine the probability of completing the project on any specific day for any specific amount of money

21. Understanding the communication model—how people effectively communicate

22. Understanding the procurement or contracting process and the project manager's role in it

Do not move on until you have mastered the key things covered in this book, and asked your team members to evaluate how well you have done.

After you have instituted improvements in your project management based on feedback from your team members, then return to this chapter to see where to go next.

Index:

A
art of project management   15
assumptions   23, 79, 110

B
benefits of a project charter   24
benefits of a work breakdown structure   101

C
change   28, 56, 74, 83
closing   14
communications management   57, 145-149, 155
communications management plan   150-151, 155
communications requirements   57-58, 146
constraints   23, 79
contingency reserve   167-169
critical path   131

D
dependency   111, 130
duration   122

E
effort   122
estimating   117, 121-125
evaluation   97
executing and controlling   14
expectations   55

H
historical information   41-44, 165
how to create a WBS   92-97, 102

I
initiating   13
issue log   68

L
lessons learned   45, 97
level of influence   54

M
management reserve   167
managing stakeholders   59
milestone   95, 110
Monte Carlo simulation   124

N
network diagram   130

O
opportunity   163, 169

P
padding   117, 121-123
planning   13
preliminary project scope statement   77
product scope   73, 77
program   36
project   33
project charter   13, 21-24
project life cycle   13, 94
project management   9

project management office   50
project management plan   14
project management process   12, 13
project management software   129-130
project scope   73, 77
project scope statement   78-80, 83

Q

qualitative risk analysis   164
quantitative risk analysis   164

R

reasons to have a project charter   24
recognition and reward systems   65
research   97
reserves   167
risk   163
risk identification   164
risk management   163-165
risk management planning   164
risk monitoring and control   164
risk register   166, 170
risk response owner   58
risk response planning   164
Rita's Process Chart   12, 181

S

schedule management   139
schedule model   131
scheduling   129, 132-133
science of project management   10
scope creep   28
sponsor   50

stakeholder identification   53-54, 59
stakeholders   22, 49-50, 54-60, 69

T
threat   163, 169
three-point estimating   123
triple constraint   15, 76

W
watchlist   169, 170
WBS dictionary   107-112, 120
work breakdown structure   89, 92, 101-102, 106, 120
work package   94-95

Notes

Notes